Fly Fishing Colorado

A No Nonsense Guide to Top Waters

Jackson Streit

NO NONSENSE

Fly Fishing Colorado

A No Nonsense Guide to Top Waters
ISBN 1-892469-13-8

© 2004 No Nonsense
Fly Fishing Guidebooks

Published by:
No Nonsense Fly Fishing Guidebooks
7493 N. Oracle Road Suite 125
Tucson, AZ 85704
(520) 547-2462
www.nononsenseguides.com

Printed in China

Editors: David Banks, Helen Condon,
   Howard Fisher
Maps, Illustrations, Design & Production:
   Pete Chadwell, Dynamic Arts
All Cover Photos by Jim Muth
Inside Photos by Jim Muth unless noted.

About the Cover

The photos on the covers are by Jim Muth, the talented photographer, guide and all around fishing pro at the Mountain Angler fly shop in Breckenridge, Colorado. Jim travels all over the state, and other places, to fish and take pictures.

The No Nonsense Creed

The best way to go fly fishing is to find out a little something about the water, and then just go. Wrong turns, surprises, self-reliance and discovering something new, even in familiar waters, are what make the memories.

The next best way is to learn enough from a local fisherman to save you from going too far wrong. You'll still find the water yourself, and it still feels as if you were the first to discover it.

This is the idea for our unique No Nonsense fly fishing series. Our books reveal little hush-hush information, yet they give all you need to find what will become your own secret places.

Painstakingly pared down, our writing is elegantly simple. Each title offers a local fly fishing expert's candid tour of favorite fly fishing waters. Nothing is oversold or out of proportion. Everything is authentic, especially the discoveries and experiences you get after using our books. In his outstanding book *Jerusalem Creek*, Ted Leeson echoes our idea.

"Discovering a new trout stream is a wonderful thing, and even if its whereabouts are common knowledge, to come upon the place yourself for the first time is nonetheless true discovery."

No Nonsense Fly Fishing Guidebooks give you a quick, clear understanding of the essential information needed to fly fish a region's most outstanding waters. The authors are highly experienced and qualified local fly fishers. Maps are tidy versions of the author's sketches.

Dedication

This guide is dedicated to my family,

Fiona, my loving wife, and Evan Taylor Streit, my son.

They make this, and most endeavors, all worthwhile.

My brother, Taylor Streit, who taught me how to fly fish. Thanks, my brother.

My mother, Eleanor Streit, who brought me into this world.

My father, Philip Streit, who has left this world yet continues to help me fish.

Table of Contents

Photos by Jim Muth.

Foreword

In 1994, at the fly fishing industry's main trade show in Denver, I was seeking someone who could put together a fly fishing guide to Colorado. My crude and unscientific market research (hunch) back then told me the world needed such a book, mostly because I really like Colorado.

Time and again at that show, fly fishing people in the know pointed to a particular fly shop in Breckenridge as a good place to find such a talent. Check in any phone book (or the back of this guide) and you'll appreciate the quantity of fly shops and fly fishing powers in Colorado. As mention of this one shop persisted, I decided I'd better find that guy.

Sure enough, Jackson Streit, the person behind The Mountain Angler in Breckenridge, turned out to be one of the best, most modest, friendliest and most talented authorities on fly fishing in Colorado one could hope to meet. After some persuasion, Jackson agreed to put everything he knew about fly fishing in his home state into a No Nonsense guidebook.

When Jackson needed additional information more specific to particular waters, he had scores of willing associates and friends across the state who were happy to contribute to his book. Often he didn't have to look much farther than the knowledgeable group in his shop, or their buddies.

The result of all this has been one of our most popular books. This is perhaps one of the happiest and most helpful fly fishing collaborations to come from college archrivals. Author Jackson is a University of Denver graduate, and the publisher is a Colorado College alum. Just attend a DU vs. CC hockey game and you will know what I mean.

David Banks

A freight train follows one of Colorado's great western rivers as an angler changes flies. Photo by Jim Muth.

Evan Streit on the Blue River. Photo by Jackson Streit.

Preface

This guidebook outlines what my angling friends and I think are the best public fly fishing waters in Colorado. Private waters are excluded, except for those that can be floated through safely by experienced boaters and those mentioned on the Rocky Mountain Angling Club pages.

Also, after a lifetime of fly fishing, I've learned that everyone has an opinion! This guide reflects mine and those of a few of my friends. You are certainly entitled to your opinion and with this guide we hope to expose you to something new to have an opinion about.

If a river or lake has been omitted, we mean no disrespect. More than likely it's not here because fewer people want to know about it. This means, however, that there might not be many people there, which isn't all bad! Additionally, if waters that are dear to you are included in this guide and you wish them less publicity, I apologize. We do feel, however, that people are entitled to the basic information in this guide. Who knows? You might meet some very interesting person as a result of this guidebook. We hope you understand.

Finally, I hope you use this guide to find a piece of fly fishing water you've always dreamed about. I think Colorado has it. And I know Colorado can offer days on the water that fulfill those dreams. Good luck!

Jackson Streit on the Colorado River. Photo by Jim Muth.

About the Author

Jackson Streit has been fly fishing for more than 33 years. Since 1971 he has fished in Colorado an average of 100 days a year!

After graduating from University of Denver, Jackson moved to the ski resort town of Breckenridge where he has lived ever since. In 1977 he started the first fly fishing guide service in the area. In 1985 he opened The Mountain Angler, a thriving fly shop he owns and operates. The shop supplies gear, guides and fly fishing information to anglers testing the many waters of Colorado…and beyond.

Jackson has personally tested those "beyond" waters, having guided and fished most of the western U.S. and Florida as well as New Zealand, Belize, Mexico, Argentina, Chile, and the Bahamas. He also escorts a group of fly fishers to Christmas Island each year.

The fly fishing community seeks Jackson, and his array of photos, for many presentations each year. He has written several articles for Colorado publications and is very involved in his Trout Unlimited chapter. In the summer, he teaches fly fishing schools.

Jackson is also passing along the family passion for fly fishing to his son Evan. When not raising a family, traveling, managing his fly shop or writing about fly fishing, Jackson plans and waits for his next chance to fish.

Acknowledgments

Although I have fished most of the waters in this guide, I recognize that there are people who are more familiar with their local waters than I. In fact they're experts and great sources of fly fishing information. So, while this guide may have my name on the cover, other experts contributed and helped ensure its accuracy. These talented, information-packed locals really know their stuff and I suggest you look them up if you're fly fishing in their area. On with the thanks.

Bud Collins, one of the top guides at Duranglers Fly Shop in Durango, and to John Flick and Tom Knopnick, owners of Duranglers. To Brad Beefus of Ross Reels, Pat Dorsey, guide for The Blue Quill Fly Shop in Evergreen. Jim Blackburn in Steamboat Springs, Bruce Keep of Vail, for his knowledge of the Eagle River. Pat Chant of Leadville, a guide for Mountain Angler, added great information on the Arkansas River. Bill Fitzsimmons contributed detailed information on the Fryingpan and Roaring Fork. Bill White from Telluride tossed in information on the San Miguel; thanks, Bill. David Padilla, former Mountain Angler manager, was also a great help. Jim Muth, photographer and expert guide, and Doug Hardwick, guide and expert bug man, both of Mountain Angler. And thanks to Kevin Macreery, for his editing and patience.

Also, thanks to my publisher David Banks, who thought me the man for the Colorado guidebook job, and Pete Chadwell, who created the maps and covers. Helen Condon, Rick Drennen and Bill Nelson, fly fishers all, provided proofreading and editing help. Thanks to all of you, and anyone I may have forgotten!

Jackson Streit

Fishing a beaver pond in the McCullough Gulch area.
Photo by Jim Muth.

Colorado Fishing Regulations and Etiquette

After more than 33 years of fly fishing in Colorado, I've formed some basic ideas that might have a bearing on your fly rodding experiences in our state.

First, we should congratulate the Colorado Division of Wildlife for its work. Over the last 30 years, the division has generally improved the quality of fly fishing in the state. An obvious example is the promotion of catch and release. Now practiced nearly everywhere in Colorado, it was a little-known department priority in the early '70s. Keep up the good work.

Second, as participation in fly fishing continues to increase almost everywhere, I suggest occasionally fly fishing lesser known or publicized waters. Though many of us would like to catch five-pound fish all day long with only a couple of buddies looking on, we do not live in Shangri-La. We live in a region, like most western states, that has only a few rivers that offer that kind of potential. That's why fly anglers are discovering the rewards of small and medium-sized streams, lakes and reservoirs that attract few, if any, anglers. These types of waters can be found throughout the Rockies, and many are described or noted in this guide. I suggest you bypass some of the major waters and give these others a try. Look for the heading "Nearby Fly Fishing" for ideas.

When driving along a popular water without finding a place to fish, consult a map or this guide. There are usually a number of nearby creeks feeding the river, lake or pond that hold fish. Getting away from the crowd, trying something new and catching a bunch of brookies or cutts isn't all that bad and is often challenging and rewarding. Most fly fishing old-timers relate with some appreciation how they learned on some small stream here or there. Fine fly fishing is not confined to the country's major tailwaters. Try a variety of waters. It will improve your skills and prove to be a lot of fun.

Third, the sheer number of anglers on the water these days brings up the etiquette issue. Years ago if another fly fisher were encountered on a stream the two would work out a plan as to who would fish where and when. Now it can be shoulder to shoulder on many waters. If this is the case, respect your fellow angler's positions. Don't crowd in on others, ever! The basic rule is: The fewer the people, the more the spacing.

Most of us love fly fishing because it is something in which we can totally immerse ourselves. It gets us away from the hustle and bustle of everyday life. I maintain that this immersion is a fascinating and enlightening hobby and the escape from routine allows us to get away from our daily insecurities and problems. This is a great rejuvenator, if not salvation.

For the many benefits that fly fishing gives us we all need to give something back. I urge you to join a local conservation group: Trout Unlimited and the Federation of Fly Fishers are a great start, or a group in your area. Believe me, with all the problems the earth is facing, the trout and salmon need our help. For all that the sport gives us, let's do something for the sport.

At whatever level you enjoy fly fishing, I urge you to please, at a minimum, follow these guidelines:

- Abide by the laws
- Respect private property
- Never crowd another angler
- Catch and release
- Carry out your litter
- Support conservation

Some Colorado Basics

Colorado freshwater game fish include rainbow, brown, golden, cutthroat, brook, lake trout, splake, Arctic grayling, kokanee salmon, northern pike, bass, crappie, sunfish, carp and bluegill.

Colorado adopted the greenback cutthroat trout as the state fish, symbolizing needed protection of the state's coldwater resources. Colorado has two cutthroat trout regions: 1) Colorado River cutthroat, one of the most colorful cutts, found throughout the high mountain areas and in the southwest corner of the state. 2) Rio Grande cutthroat, with most of its spots near the tail, inhabits south-central Colorado.

The cutthroat, not the rainbow, originally populated most of the West. Geologic forces corralled some thirteen species into distinct regions. Cutthroats were named because of the large, bright red marking below the jaw.

Colorado has most insects that fly fishers recognize. Mysis shrimp, uncommon in the West, is found in Colorado lakes and reservoirs. This pearl-white freshwater shrimp is similar to a scud. It is usually washed from stillwater into a stream (usually tailwaters). There are three main Mysis shrimp patterns; the most popular is Liquia-Lace.

Cheesman Canyon on the South Platte River.
Photo by Jim Muth.

Colorful cutthroat trout from the Middle Fork South Platte River. Photo by Jim Muth.

One can combine fly fishing and skiing at one of Colorado's twenty-five ski areas in the same trip. Colorado has fifty-six peaks 14,000 feet above sea level, or more. (There are only about sixty "Fourteeners" in the U.S.) Often in Colorado, you are at a higher elevation than in many places in the United States. A step at the Colorado state capitol in Denver is exactly 5,280 feet above sea level. High altitude affects most people. When visiting Colorado, take a day or two to get acclimated. Replenish fluids. Protect against too much sun.

It can snow any day of the year in Colorado. Afternoon lightning, gusts and rain are common in spring and summer, so always take a windbreaker, parka, a hat, and extra dry clothing. Take good equipment and an area map when hiking or backpacking into high mountain lakes. Leave your itinerary with someone.

How to Use This Book

This guide was assembled from information I've compiled during the 30 plus years I've fly fished in Colorado. Blended into my observations is the expertise of other talented people who fish the fly in the Rockies. The combination is nuts and bolts "expert" advice. While some consider me an expert, I maintain that when fly fishing I'm also a pupil, always learning. Thus the information in this guide (or any other Colorado guide) is not the final word on the subject. The subject moves, conditions change and experts keep learning. I'm sure those who have contributed to this guide agree on this. And, as Idaho outfitter Bill Mason observed, it is rare and significant when fly fishing people agree on much of anything.

So keep in mind that the information in this guide is a precise overview from "experts" who continue to learn. This No Nonsense guide is a quick, clear outline of the best fly fishing in Colorado. Read this guide, then go fly fishing in our state. You'll keep learning and you'll love it!

Information

Colorado is a big place. There are a number of quality fly fishing specialty stores in the state and most offer a guide service. (Most of these shops are listed in the back of this book.) These shops and guides are valuable sources of information. Talk to these people; odds are they know exactly what is happening on the water on any given day. This information, from some pretty nice folks, can make your fly fishing trip the best. Contact them.

Regulations

Always pick up a copy of the Colorado Fishing Season Information and Wildlife Property Directory before you go fishing and check the latest rules from Colorado Division of Wildlife (303-297-1192). In Colorado, regs are set for three years. The regulations that apply to the waters described here are reliable. Over time, most haven't changed much, but undoubtedly there are some late revisions or alterations we haven't been able to get in this book. Check with the state first. (Colorado Division of Wildlife recorded message, Stocking Report: 303-291-7534.)

Colorado Gold Medal Waters

Gold Medal Waters offer the greatest potential for trophy trout fishing and angling success and usually have special regulations. Gold Medal Waters in this guide include: The Blue, Colorado, Fryingpan, Gunnison, North Platte, Rio Grande, Roaring Fork, South Platte (middle and south forks) rivers, Gore Creek, North Delaney Lake and Spinney Mountain Reservoir. Designations can change and don't necessarily mean that other waters don't fish as well.

Colorado Wild Trout Waters

These waters support self-sustaining trout populations and are stocked only in emergencies. These include sections of the following: The Animas, Blue, Cache La Poudre, Colorado, Conejos, Lake Fork of the Gunnison, East River, Laramie, Fraser, Gunnison, South Platte, Middle Fork of the South Platte, North Platte and Roaring Fork rivers, Cascade, Cochetopa,

Colorado River. Photo by Jim Muth.

Bob Voth with a big rainbow from the Middle Fork South Platte River. Photo by Jim Muth.

Los Pinos, North St. Vrain, Osier and Tarryall creeks, Emerald, Steamboat and Trappers lakes.

Ratings

Ratings range from 1 to 10. A "1" is un-fishable, a "5" is fair, and a rating of "10" means the highest quality fly fishing experience in Colorado.

This guide highlights waters rated five and above. The ratings reflect my experience (plus those of my contributors) gained over many years and allow for seasonal problems, water conditions, etc. Use these ratings as a rough guide and comparison to your experience and those of your fly fishing friends.

Private Land

You must obtain permission to fish on private property in Colorado. If you don't, you can lose your license. Historically, in Colorado the property owner owns the river bottom. Fly fishers cannot cross onto private property just because they were in the water or because they stayed below the high water mark.

In Colorado, you can float through private property if you enter the river on public land and leave the river on public land. Or, you can enter and exit the water on private land if you receive permission from the landowner. You cannot stop, leave the boat, and touch bottom, anchor or beach if you are on private land. Check at a local fly shop or read the Division of Wildlife regulations.

Hatches

We've listed the major hatches known for each water. This may change with conditions and fly fishers, so information here is general. From a local fly shop it's gospel. In most cases try to offer something that matches the hatch.

Common Colorado Game Fish

Illustrations by Joseph R. Tomelleri.

Rainbow Trout

Brown Trout

Colorado Cutthroat Trout

Rio Grande Cutthroat Trout

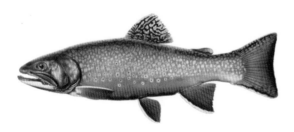

Brook Trout

Lake Trout

Arctic Grayling

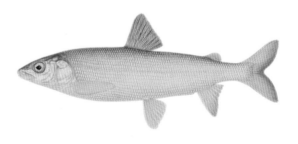

Mountain Whitefish

Northern Pike

Walleye Pike

Largemouth Bass

Smallmouth Bass

Black Crappie

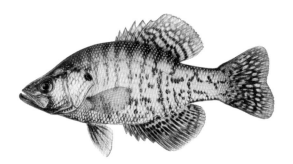

White Crappie

Kokanee Salmon (spawning male)

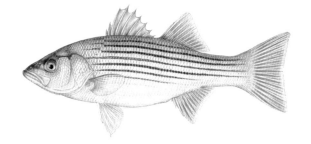

Striped Bass

Flies to Use in Colorado

Adams Parachute

Royal Wulff

Comparadun

Elk Hair Caddis

Red Quill

Melon Quill

Colorado Green Drake

Hacklewing Green Drake

Humpy

Lime Trude

Yellow Stimulator

Convertible

Schroeder's Parachute Hopper

Trailing Shuck Midge

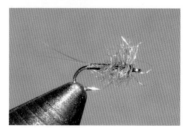

Triple-Wing Trico Spinner

Midge Biot

Barr's Emerger
(PMD, BWO, Trico)

WD-40

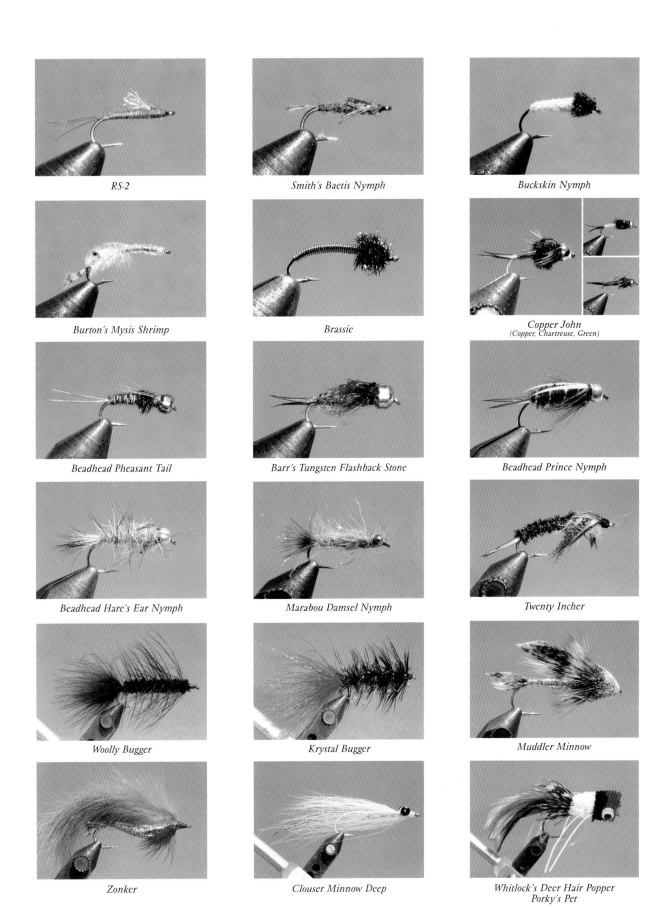

RS-2

Smith's Baetis Nymph

Buckskin Nymph

Burton's Mysis Shrimp

Brassie

Copper John
(Copper, Chartreuse, Green)

Beadhead Pheasant Tail

Barr's Tungsten Flashback Stone

Beadhead Prince Nymph

Beadhead Hare's Ear Nymph

Marabou Damsel Nymph

Twenty Incher

Woolly Bugger

Krystal Bugger

Muddler Minnow

Zonker

Clouser Minnow Deep

Whitlock's Deer Hair Popper
Porky's Pet

Photos by Pete Chadwell.

19

Conditions by the Month

Here are general conditions for fly fishing waters in Colorado by month. You can use this list to help plan your vacation to Colorado. Or, if you are in the state, a quick glance at this listing will show you where to fish, given the time of the year. Always consult the local fly shops to get the latest information.

Legend: ☐ Not Fishable   ▨ Fair   ▩ Good   ■ Prime

	Jan	Feb	Mar	Apr	May	Jun	Jul	Aug	Sep	Oct	Nov	Dec
Animas River												
Arkansas River												
Big Thompson River												
Blue River												
Cache La Poudre River												
Colorado River												
Conejos River												
Delaney Butte Lakes												
Dolores River												
Eagle River												
Fryingpan River												
Grand Mesa Area												
Gunnison River												
High Alpine Lakes												
North Platte River												
Piedra River												
Rio Grande												
Roaring Fork River												
San Miguel River												
South Platte/Deckers												
South Platte/South Park												
Spinney Mountain Reservoir												
Taylor River												
Trappers Lake												
Yampa River												

Mount Massive looms over an angler on the Arkansas River.
Photo by Jim Muth.

Top Colorado
Fly Fishing Waters

Above: Happy high altitude anglers in Colorado.
Facing page: Tug-of-war with an Eagle River trout.
Photos by Jim Muth.

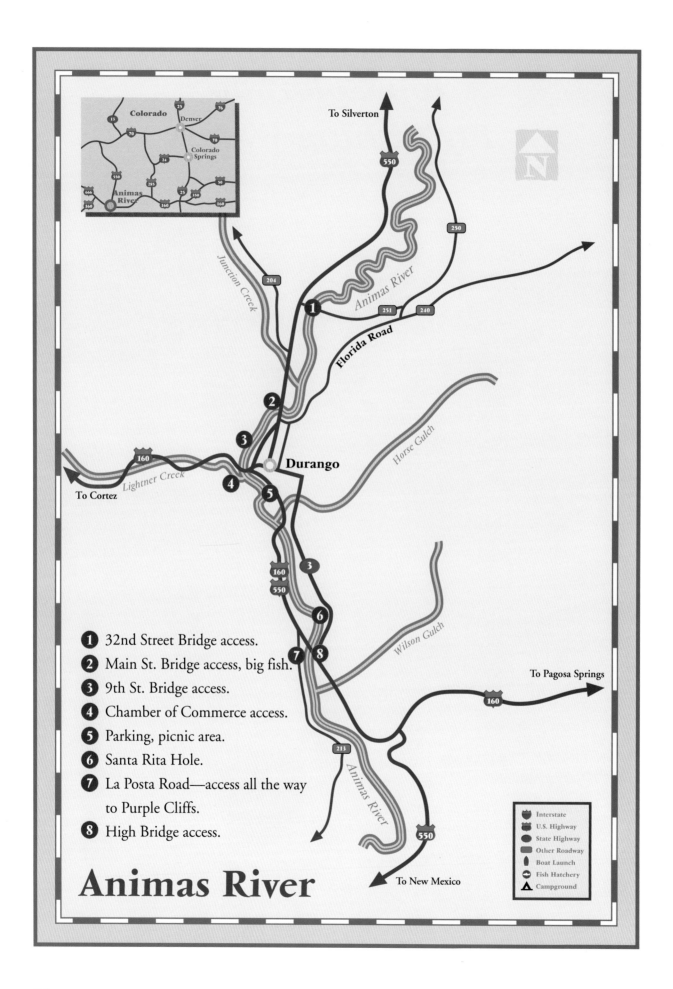

1 32nd Street Bridge access.

2 Main St. Bridge access, big fish.

3 9th St. Bridge access.

4 Chamber of Commerce access.

5 Parking, picnic area.

6 Santa Rita Hole.

7 La Posta Road—access all the way to Purple Cliffs.

8 High Bridge access.

Animas River

Legend:
- Interstate
- U.S. Highway
- State Highway
- Other Roadway
- Boat Launch
- Fish Hatchery
- Campground

To Silverton

To Cortez

Durango

To Pagosa Springs

To New Mexico

Animas River

Florida Road

Horse Gulch

Wilson Gulch

Junction Creek

Lightner Creek

Colorado
Denver
Colorado Springs
Animas River

Animas River

The Animas River is large by southwest Colorado standards (100 feet wide in some places) and there is no dam interrupting its flow from Silverton to Farmington, New Mexico. The narrow gauge Durango & Silverton Railroad runs through the scenic canyons and along the upper river from June to August. (Make reservations six weeks in advance.) The water here is fast with riffles and pools.

Mining operations have contaminated some of the upper river with heavy metals. Fortunately, by the time the river flows through the city of Durango it's been diluted by feeder streams and is a fine fishery.

Starting about nine miles north of Durango the river meanders and in places is deep, slow, large, open and generally windy. There's public access to the river through the city and three miles downstream to the Purple Cliffs below town.

Water for the Animas comes from a huge drainage area and is affected by snowmelt and summer storms. During heavy snow years the Animas may not clear until July and can be high and roily throughout the Caddis hatches.

To get to the Animas, head to southern Colorado and either make your way to Highway 160, which runs east to west, or take scenic Highway 550, which runs north to south. Both get you to Durango, but the latter runs along the upper section of the river.

A strong brown trout from the Animas River. Photo by Brian O'Keefe.

Types of Fish
Brown, rainbow and a few cutthroat and brookies. Fish 18–20 inches are taken.

Known Hatches
November-March: Midges (Diptera).
April-May, late August-November: Blue-Winged Olives (Baetis).
Late April-July: Caddis (various).
May: Stoneflies (Dark Giant Stone, Pteronarcys californica), Willowflies (Acroneuria pacifica).
Mid-July to early August: Green Drake (Ephemerella grandis).

Equipment to Use
Rods: 5-7 weight, 9-9 1/2'.
Reels: Click and pawl or disc with a good drag.
Line: Heavier floating and sink tip (for streamers) to match rod weight.
Leaders: 2x to 5x, 9'.
Wading: Tough wading here. Use breathable, chest-high waders, boots with cleats and a wading staff. Lightweight waders work well in summer heat.

Flies to Use
Dries: Elk Hair Caddis, Wulff, Humpy, Irresistible & Trude #12-16, Green Drakes #12 (during hatches), Sofa Pillow, Stimulator #6-12 (for Stonefly and Willowfly hatches).
Nymphs & Streamers: Hare's Ear #10-14, all colors Copper John #14-20, Prince & Beadhead #8-16, Caddis Larva & Pupa #12-16, Beadhead Barr's Emerger BWO #16-22, Bird's Stone, Halfback #6-12, Twenty Incher #6-10, Woolly Bugger #2/0 - 4, Clouser Minnow, Sculpin #2/0 - 2.

When to Fish
Heavy runoff usually lasts until mid-June, so the river starts fishing very well when it is high and clearing. Durango summers are warm and midday fishing is slow. Things really pick up in the fall when browns are spawning. The Animas is also a good winter fishery with a surprising number of moderate days. Water temperature near 40° usually means good fishing.

Seasons & Limits
Open year-round. From Lightner Creek to Purple Cliffs, Gold Medal Water & artificial flies and lures only. The bag and possession limit for trout is two fish, 16" or longer.

Nearby Fly Fishing
The Dolores, Piedra, Florida and San Juan rivers.

Accommodations & Services
Durango has a variety of motels, hotels and restaurants as well as other services. You can actually fish out of some of the motels in town.

Rating
Chances of landing a real trophy are as good here as any place in western Colorado. The Animas rates an 8.5.

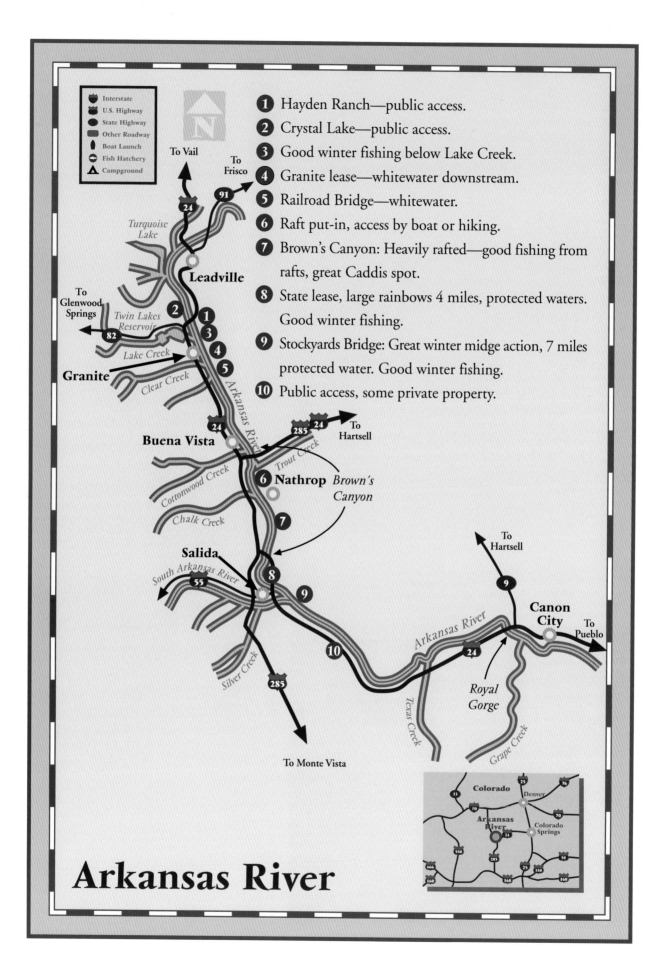

Legend

- Interstate
- U.S. Highway
- State Highway
- Other Roadway
- Boat Launch
- Fish Hatchery
- ▲ Campground

N

To Vail

To Frisco

91

Turquoise Lake

24

Leadville

To Glenwood Springs

2

1

82

Twin Lakes Reservoir

3

Lake Creek

4

Granite

5

Clear Creek

Arkansas River

24

Buena Vista

285 **24**

To Hartsell

Cottonwood Creek

Trout Creek

6 **Nathrop** *Brown's Canyon*

Chalk Creek

7

To Hartsell

Salida

South Arkansas River

8

9

55

9

Canon City

To Pueblo

Arkansas River

Silver Creek

10

24

285

Royal Gorge

Texas Creek

Grape Creek

To Monte Vista

1. Hayden Ranch—public access.
2. Crystal Lake—public access.
3. Good winter fishing below Lake Creek.
4. Granite lease—whitewater downstream.
5. Railroad Bridge—whitewater.
6. Raft put-in, access by boat or hiking.
7. Brown's Canyon: Heavily rafted—good fishing from rafts, great Caddis spot.
8. State lease, large rainbows 4 miles, protected waters. Good winter fishing.
9. Stockyards Bridge: Great winter midge action, 7 miles protected water. Good winter fishing.
10. Public access, some private property.

Colorado

25 **76**

Denver

13

70

Arkansas River

70

Colorado Springs

24

550

285

50

666

160

25

350

160

160

Arkansas River

Arkansas River

The "Ark" is a relatively under-fished river, known for a prolific May to June Caddis hatch. Many other hatches combine to make this a true western "big water" fly fishing experience.

The mountain section flows 150 miles from the old mining town of Climax through central Colorado to the Pueblo Reservoir. From 12,000-foot elevation at the Continental Divide, it drops to 4,700 feet in the eastern plains. There are hundreds of year-round fly fishing opportunities, especially below Lake Creek and from Salida to Pueblo.

The recent acquisition of the Hayden Ranch Recreation Area adds another 5.8 miles of public water access to the Arkansas. Located just south of Leadville, Hayden Ranch is quickly becoming a favorite of the knowledgeable angler.

There are numerous rafters, termed "the rubber hatch" by local anglers, May to August.

The Brown's Canyon and Royal Gorge runs are particularly popular.

Fishing from boats can be quite successful especially when casting streamers at the banks and behind structure. Boaters need knowledge of class III-V water. Contact a qualified guide if you're new to river rafting.

Arkansas River brook trout. Photo by Jim Muth.

Types of Fish
Predominantly reproducing brown trout with some rainbow and cutthroat that average 11–14 inches.

Known Hatches
July to early September: PMD (Ephemerella infrequens & inermis). *July to mid-September:* Upper river, Red Quill (Rhithrogena hageni). *Late March to early July & mid-September to November:* BWO (Baetis), Caddis (Brachycentrus), prolific hatch late-April near Pueblo going up river until early July. *June to September:* Caddis (various, sporadic). *November to May:* Midges (Diptera). *Mid-June to early July:* Golden Stoneflies (Acroneuria pacifica). *Mid-June to August:* Upper river, Little Yellow Sally (Isoperla).

Equipment to Use
Rods: 4-6 weight, 8 1/2-9'.
Reels: Disc or palm drag.
Line: Floating and sink tip to match rod weight.
Leaders: 3x to 6x, 8-10' to match conditions.
Wading: Chest waders with felt-soled boots. Wading staff during runoff, May to early July.

Flies to Use
Dries, January-March: Griffith's Gnat, Puterbaugh's Midge, Stalcup's & Betts Midge Emerger #20-24, Grizzly Midge #20-22. *Late March:* Baetis Parachute, No-hackle BWO, Stalcup's CDC Comparadun BWO #20-22, Blue Dun #18. *April-May:* Previous Midges, Baetis, plus Grey Bodied Elk Hair Caddis and Hemingway Caddis #16-18. *June-July:* Orange & Yellow Stimulators #8-12 for Stoneflies. *June-September:* Previous Baetis & Caddis patterns, Pale Morning Dun, Light & Pink Cahill, Melon & Red Quill, Stalcup's CDC Red Quill Comparadun & Mahogany Dun #14-18. *October-December:* Previous Midge and Baetis. *Terrestrials & Attractors, June-September:* Dave's, Joe's & Schroeder's Hoppers #8-14, Ant, Beetle, Cricket #12-16, Humpy, Wulff, Irresistible #14-18. *Nymphs:* Hare's Ear, Caddis Larva #10-16, Pheasant Tail, Copper John #14-20, Chant's Beadhead, Beadhead Prince #8-16, Bread Crust, Sparkle Caddis Pupa, Colorado & Barr's Net Building Caddis #12-16, Golden Stone #8-10, Midge Larva #18-22, Beadhead Barr's Emerger BWO #16-22.

When to Fish
Dry fly fishing is excellent May to mid-September and really exciting during the Caddis hatch May to June. Some canyon waters can freeze in winter.

Seasons & Limits
Regulations are quite varied along the course of the Ark. Consult current regulations or a fly shop.

Nearby Fly Fishing
The South Fork of the Arkansas, South Platte, Eagle, Blue and Taylor rivers. Ten Mile, Rock, Lake, Clear, Trout, Halfmoon and Chalk creeks. Emerald, Twin and Turquoise lakes and Clear Creek Reservoir.

Accommodations & Services
Leadville, Buena Vista, Salida and Canon City have motels, hotels, restaurants, markets and tackle.

Rating
Smaller fish, but greater numbers and relatively light fishing pressure combine for a 7.5.

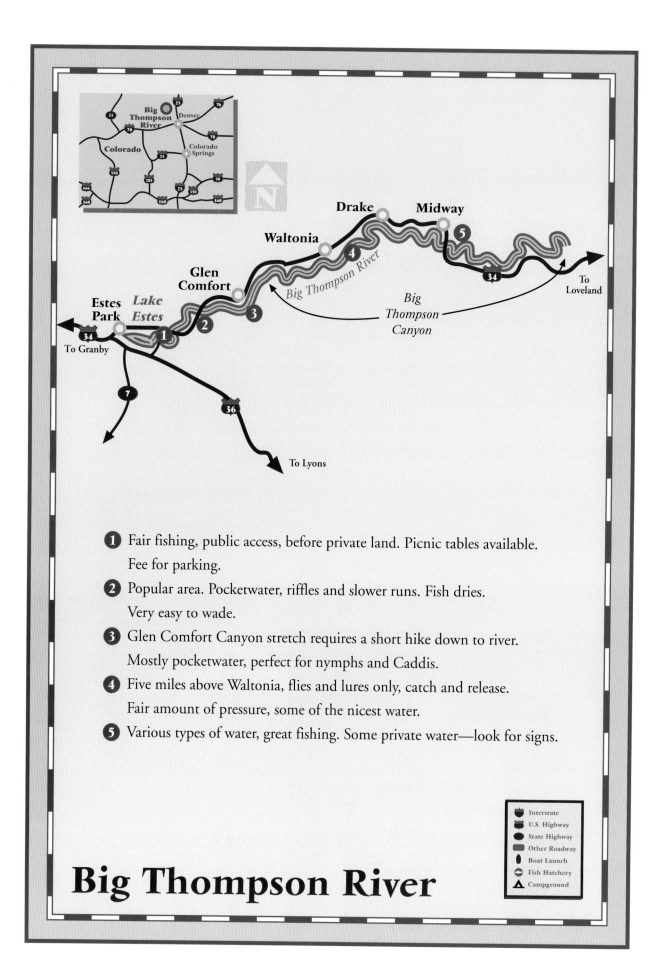

❶ Fair fishing, public access, before private land. Picnic tables available. Fee for parking.

❷ Popular area. Pocketwater, riffles and slower runs. Fish dries. Very easy to wade.

❸ Glen Comfort Canyon stretch requires a short hike down to river. Mostly pocketwater, perfect for nymphs and Caddis.

❹ Five miles above Waltonia, flies and lures only, catch and release. Fair amount of pressure, some of the nicest water.

❺ Various types of water, great fishing. Some private water—look for signs.

Big Thompson River

Interstate
U.S. Highway
State Highway
Other Roadway
Boat Launch
Fish Hatchery
Campground

Big Thompson River

From high in Rocky Mountain National Park in north central Colorado, the Big Thompson flows east through a canyon to the town of Loveland and eventually into the plains, where it meets the South Platte near Greeley.

Starting small, the Big Thompson becomes a medium-sized meadow river after it leaves the heavily fished Lake Estes (in the town of Estes Park) and Big Thompson Canyon.

The river is subject to low flows and ice during the winter months, which makes fishing tough or sometimes impossible. There's some fantastic dry fly fishing, however, starting in spring and continuing to early fall.

To access the Big Thompson from the east, get on Interstate 25 going north to Loveland. Then take Highway 34 west to Estes Park. This highway runs along the river where you'll encounter the meadow section, then the canyon, then Estes Lake.

The Big Thompson flows through some beautiful scenery starting in Colorado's Rocky Mountain National Park. Photo by Quang-Tuan Luong, Terra Galleria Photography.

Types of Fish
Stocked rainbow, cutthroat, and wild brown trout. There are also naturally reproducing browns and rainbows. Fish average 6-14 inches.

Known Hatches
February-May: Midges (Diptera).
Late April-June: Stoneflies (various).
May-September: Caddis (various).
March-October: Blue-Winged Olives (Baetis).
July-August: Pale Morning Duns (Ephemerella inermis, infrequens).
July-August: Green Drakes (Ephemerella grandis).
August-September: Red Quills (Rhithrogena hageni).

Equipment to Use
Rods: 2-5 weight, 7 1/2-9'.
Reels: Disc or mechanical drag.
Line: Floating to match rod weight.
Leaders: 4x to 6x, 9' for dries, 7 1/2 to 9' for nymphs.
Wading: The entire length of river is very accessible except during spring runoff. Breathable waders with felt-soled boots are best; hippers are fine in late summer/fall.

Flies to Use
Dries: Match above hatches with Midge adults #18-24, also Griffith's Gnat #20-22, Renegade, Elk Hair Caddis, Humpy, Wulff #14-18, Adams #14-20, Stimulator #8-14, Green Drake #12, Comparadun, Pale Morning Dun #16-18, Lime & Pink Trude and Rio Grande King Trude, Red Quill #14-16, Blue-Winged Olive #16-22. *Nymphs:* Beadhead Prince, Chamois #14-16, all colors Copper John #14-20, Beadhead Hare's Ear, Flashback Pheasant Tail #12-18, Beadhead Barr's Emerger BWO #16-22, Brassies #18-20, Palomino Midge #18-22, Stone #12-14, Woolly Bugger #4-6.

When to Fish
Starting in mid-April until runoff (mid-May to mid-June in most years) fly fishing is quite good. Excellent dry fly fishing starts late June and lasts until mid-October.

Seasons & Limits
Fish year-round. From the bridge at Waltonia upstream 5.3 miles to the bridge at Noel's Draw (Common Point or Estes Park Gun Range) fishing with artificial flies and lures only. All landed fish must be returned to the water immediately.

Nearby Fly Fishing
North Fork of the Big Thompson, Lake Estes, Mary's Lake, St. Vrain Creek.

Accommodations & Services
Services of all kinds are available in Estes Park (Chamber of Commerce 970-586-4431). Camping throughout the area in designated areas only.

Rating
When fishing well, just before and after runoff until October, this river rates a 7.

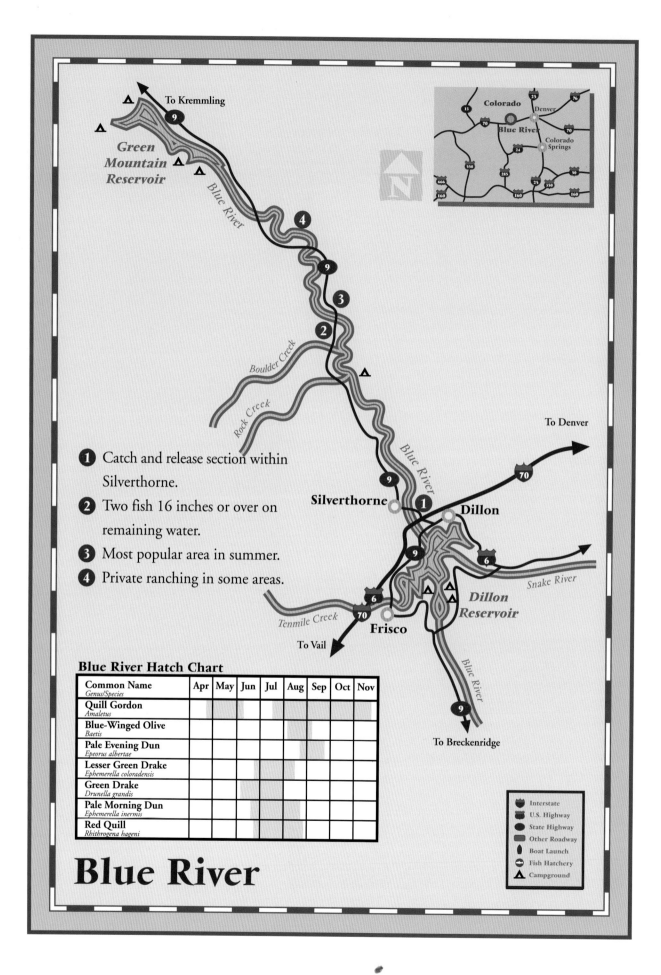

To Kremmling

Green Mountain Reservoir

Blue River

Boulder Creek

Rock Creek

To Denver

① Catch and release section within Silverthorne.

② Two fish 16 inches or over on remaining water.

③ Most popular area in summer.

④ Private ranching in some areas.

Silverthorne

Dillon

Blue River

Snake River

Dillon Reservoir

Tenmile Creek

Frisco

To Vail

Blue River

To Breckenridge

Blue River Hatch Chart

Common Name *Genus/Species*	Apr	May	Jun	Jul	Aug	Sep	Oct	Nov
Quill Gordon *Amaletus*								
Blue-Winged Olive *Baetis*								
Pale Evening Dun *Epeorus albertae*								
Lesser Green Drake *Ephemerella coloradensis*								
Green Drake *Drunella grandis*								
Pale Morning Dun *Ephemerella inermis*								
Red Quill *Rhithrogena hageni*								

Blue River

Colorado
Denver
Blue River
Colorado Springs

Interstate
U.S. Highway
State Highway
Other Roadway
Boat Launch
Fish Hatchery
Campground

Blue River

The Blue is a medium-size river, running 100-300 cfs most years, and one of the most scenic Gold Medal fisheries in Colorado. Fly fish from Dillon Reservoir dam down to the Colorado River. From Dillon to Green Mountain Reservoir offers the best chance for success. Much of the other water is private, so most anglers use the ten miles of public access between the two lakes.

Below Dillon Reservoir dam in the town of Silverthorne is the most popular year-round tailwater in the area, especially for large fish. Big trout live here because of the abundance of Mysis shrimp coming from the reservoir. There is excellent winter midge fishing in this section. The river freezes over downstream at about the five-mile mark starting in mid to late December. Late March to November the entire river fishes well. Look for runoff conditions downstream mid-May to mid-June.

River access is clearly marked by Division of Wildlife signs and at parking areas. There are also National Forest easements. Colorado Highway 9 parallels the river.

A quiet run on the Blue River. Photo by Jim Muth.

Types of Fish
Brown, rainbow, some brook trout, cutthroats and fall spawning Kokanee salmon.

Known Hatches
January-February: Midges (Diptera). *March-April:* Midges, Snowflies (Capnia), Baetis. *May:* Baetis, Caddis. *June:* Caddis, PMD (Ephemerella inermis), Golden Stone (Acroneuria pacifica), Salmonflies (Pteronarcys californica). *July:* Caddis, PMD, Baetis, Green Drake (Ephemerella grandis), Red Quill (Rhithrogena hageni), Yellow Sally (Isoperla). *August:* Caddis, Baetis, Yellow Sally, Lesser Green Drake (Ephemerella coloradensis), Pale Evening Dun (Epeorus albertae). *September:* Caddis, Baetis, Lesser Green Drake. *October-December:* Baetis, Midges.

Equipment to Use
Rods: 3-6 weight, 8-9'. *Line:* Floating line to match. *Leaders:* 4x to 7x, 9 - 10'.
Wading: Chest-high waders with felt-soled boots. Studs can help. Hippers OK in late summer.

Flies to Use
December-February: Midge & Emerger, Griffith's Gnat #18-24, Trailing Shuck Midge, Snowfly #18-22. *March-April:* Black Micro Caddis, Baetis #18-20, Midge and Trailing Shuck. *May-June:* Elk Hair Caddis #16-18, Stonefly #18-22, Sofa Pillow #4-8, Orange Stimulator #6-10, PMD, Light & Pink Cahill, Melon Quill #16. *July-August:* PMD, Light & Pink Cahill #14-16, Melon Quill #16, Red Quill, Rusty Spinner, Adams & Adams Parachute #14-18, Green Drake #10-12, Baetis #18-20, Schroeder's Para-Hopper #10-14, Elk Hair Caddis #12-18. *September-October:* Previous attractor dries plus Hoppers #10-12, BWO #16-22, Adams Parachute #16-20, Baetis Parachute #18-22. *November:* Baetis, Blue Dun #16-22, Midges #18-22. *Nymphs:* Pheasant Tail #14-22, Hare's Ear #12-20, all colors Copper John #14-20, Midge Larva, WD 40 #18-22, Mysis Shrimp #14-18, Golden Stone #8, Beadhead Hare's Ear #14-16, Prince Beadhead, Green Drake #10-12, Barr's Emerger #16-20, Brassies #18-20, RS-2, Beadhead Barr's Emerger BWO #16-22.

When to Fish
The upper river: fall and winter. *Lower river above Green Mountain Reservoir:* April-May and July-Sept. Runoff discoloration mid-May to mid-June.

Seasons & Limits (Check at fly shop)
Artificial flies and lures only, open year-round except above Dillon Reservoir: closed Oct. to Feb. 1. Catch and release in Silverthorne. Downstream to Colorado River, limit two trout, 16 inches plus.

Nearby Fly Fishing
Colorado, Eagle, South Platte, Swan and Arkansas rivers and Ten Mile, Rock, Slate, Boulder and Williams Fork creeks.

Accommodations & Services
Campgrounds around Dillon and Green Mountain Reservoirs and on the river six miles north of Silverthorne. All services in Dillon, Frisco, Silverthorne and Breckenridge.

Rating
A year-round fishery, a chance to catch a lunker in the Mysis-rich tailwater, the Blue is a solid 7.

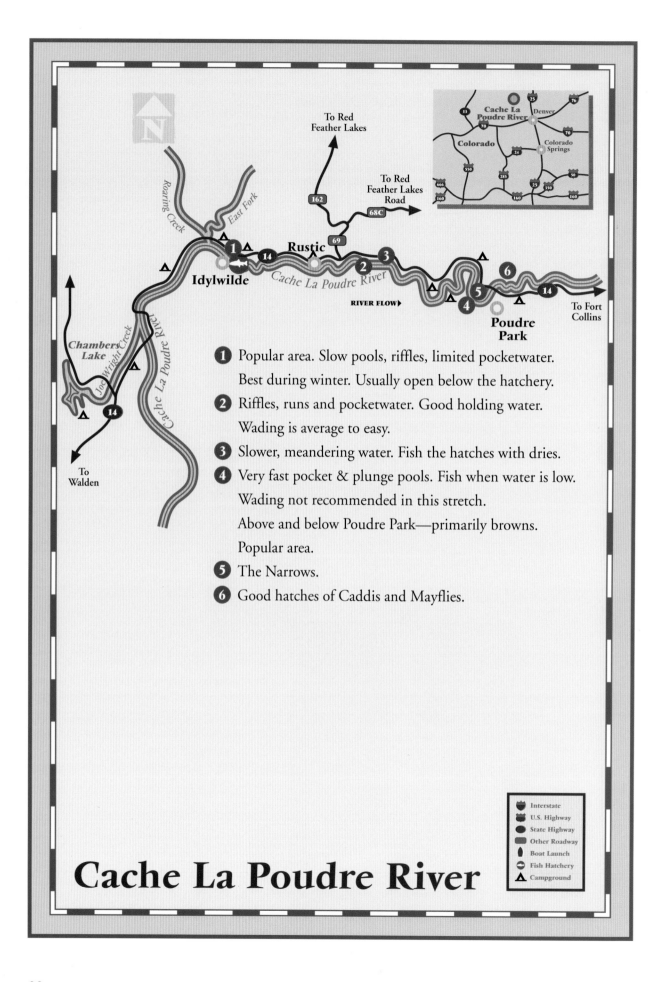

N

To Red
Feather Lakes

To Red
Feather Lakes
Road

162

68C

69

Rustic

1

14

Idylwilde

East Fork

Roaring Creek

Cache La Poudre River

3

2

RIVER FLOW▶

6

5

4

14

To Fort
Collins

Poudre
Park

Chambers
Lake

Joe Wright Creek

Cache La Poudre River

14

To
Walden

Cache La
Poudre River

Colorado

Denver

Colorado
Springs

25

76

13

70

70

550

21

285

25

350

50

160

666

160

160

❶ Popular area. Slow pools, riffles, limited pocketwater.
Best during winter. Usually open below the hatchery.

❷ Riffles, runs and pocketwater. Good holding water.
Wading is average to easy.

❸ Slower, meandering water. Fish the hatches with dries.

❹ Very fast pocket & plunge pools. Fish when water is low.
Wading not recommended in this stretch.
Above and below Poudre Park—primarily browns.
Popular area.

❺ The Narrows.

❻ Good hatches of Caddis and Mayflies.

Interstate
U.S. Highway
State Highway
Other Roadway
Boat Launch
Fish Hatchery
Campground

Cache La Poudre River

Cache La Poudre River

The Poudre is one of the larger freestone rivers draining out of the Rockies onto the plains of northern Colorado. It is also one of the last remaining rivers along the Front Range without a dam or reservoir. It offers a variety of water types and has an excellent insect population that provides prolific hatches.

There are approximately forty-seven fishable miles of "upper" and "lower" mountain water. The upper headwaters, near the national park, average twenty five feet wide, offer some of the best fly fishing and require a hike or 4WD.

The lower section is easily accessed along Colorado Highway 14, which parallels much of the river. This convenience, and nearby Fort Collins and Greeley, make for a fair amount of fishing pressure.

Scouting the North Fork of the Poudre River. Photo by Brian O'Keefe.

Types of Fish
Rainbow, brown, and some cutthroat.

Known Hatches
March-November: Midges (Diptera). *April-June:* Stoneflies (various). *April-October:* Blue-Winged Olives (Baetis). *May-September:* Caddis (various). *July-August:* Pale Morning Duns (Ephemerella inermis). *August:* Red Quills (Rhithrogena hageni). *August-October:* Tricos.

Equipment to Use
Rods: 2-5 weight, 7 1/2-9'.
Reels: Mechanical or disc drag.
Line: Floating to match rod weight.
Leaders: 5x-7x, 9' for dries, 7 1/2 to 9' for nymphs.
Wading: Chest-high waders with felt-soled boots. Upper stretches are relatively easy; the Narrows are impossible even during low water.

Flies to Use
Dries: Match the above hatches using Stalcup's Midge Emerger, Griffith's Gnat, Betts Midge Emerger #20-22, Barr's Emerger, Adams Parachute #16-20, Adams #14-20, Blue-Winged Olive, Trico Spinner #18-22, Rusty Spinner #16, Elk Hair Caddis, Wulff, Humpies, Irresistible and Trudes #14-18, Stimulator #8-14, Red & Light Cahill, PMD Comparadun #16-18. *Nymphs & Streamers:* Beadhead Prince and Hare's Ear #16-18, Beadhead Barr's Emerger BWO #16-22, all colors Copper John #14-20, Beadhead Pheasant Tail #16-20, Brassies #18-20, Midge Larva #18-22, Caddis Larva #14-16, Muddler Minnow, Woolly Bugger #4-6.

When to Fish
Fish good Caddis hatches before runoff (late April to mid-May). Quality fishing returns June to early November when the fish slow down. December to January, the river is generally frozen and un-fishable. Midge activity is best February - March.

Seasons & Limits
Fly fish year-round. Wild Trout Water, not shown on map, is from the Pingree Park Road/bridge upstream to the west boundary of the Hombre Ranch (just below Rustic) and from Black Hollow Creek upstream to and including Big Bend campground. Use artificial flies and lures only. The bag and possession limit for trout is two fish, 16" or longer. Artificial flies and lures only in the following sections: Rocky Mountain Park boundary down to Joe Wright Creek, North Fork of the Poudre, from Bull Creek (above Halligan Reservoir) upstream to Divide Creek. Return all fish to the water immediately.

Nearby Fly Fishing
The Laramie and North Platte rivers. Sheep, Pennock, Buckhorn and Roaring Fork creeks and Zimmerman Lake.

Accommodations & Services
Fort Collins has all services (Chamber of Commerce 970-482-3746). There are some cabins and stores along Highway 14 and many campgrounds along the river.

Rating
Close to town, miles of public access and strong hatches, this freestone river rates a strong 7.

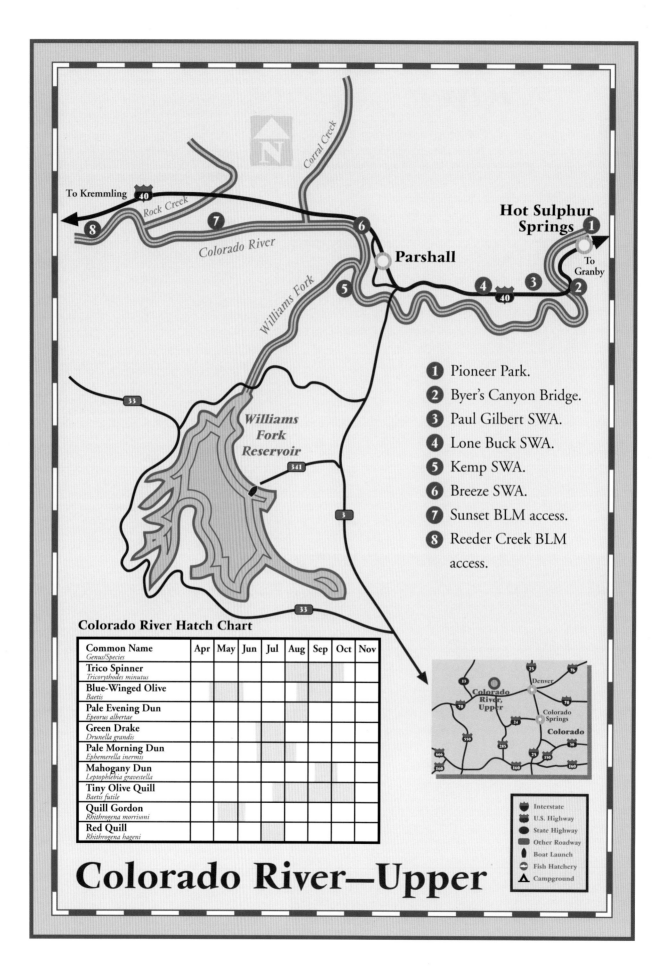

Colorado River—Upper

To Kremmling
Hot Sulphur Springs
To Granby
Parshall
Corral Creek
Rock Creek
Colorado River
Williams Fork
Williams Fork Reservoir

1 Pioneer Park.
2 Byer's Canyon Bridge.
3 Paul Gilbert SWA.
4 Lone Buck SWA.
5 Kemp SWA.
6 Breeze SWA.
7 Sunset BLM access.
8 Reeder Creek BLM access.

Colorado River Hatch Chart

Common Name *Genus/Species*	Apr	May	Jun	Jul	Aug	Sep	Oct	Nov
Trico Spinner *Tricorythodes minutus*								
Blue-Winged Olive *Baetis*								
Pale Evening Dun *Epeorus albertae*								
Green Drake *Drunella grandis*								
Pale Morning Dun *Ephemerella inermis*								
Mahogany Dun *Leptophlebia gravestella*								
Tiny Olive Quill *Baetis futile*								
Quill Gordon *Rhithrogena morrisoni*								
Red Quill *Rhithrogena hageni*								

Colorado River, Upper
Denver
Colorado Springs
Colorado

Interstate
U.S. Highway
State Highway
Other Roadway
Boat Launch
Fish Hatchery
Campground

Colorado River— Upper
Hot Sulphur Springs to Kremmling

This section is not as big and mighty as stretches farther downstream and one can wade across the river in most areas. This section probably fishes better than the others and there are plenty of State Wildlife Area (SWA) access and parking. In all, a great example of a large and long western-type fly fishing stream.

The Kemp and Breeze SWAs (below Parshall) have excellent hatches and some large fish. Upstream, the Lone Buck and Paul Gilbert SWAs are also very good spots to fish.

The Williams Fork tailwater provides year-round fly fishing. The section below the Williams Fork and Colorado River confluence is open most of the winter but cannot be drifted. Flows: 175-400 cfs. Most of the water below the Sunset BLM lease passes through private property. Fish the Gore Canyon area instead (see Middle Section following). To reach the upper section, go east from Kremmling on Highway 40. You'll see accesses from the highway.

Upper Colorado River near Parshall. Photo by Jim Muth.

Types of Fish
Rainbow and brown trout, Colorado River cutbows, a few brookies and cutthroats.

Known Hatches
January-April: Midges (Diptera). *May:* Golden Stone (Acroneuria pacifica), Baetis, Quill Gordon (Rhithrogena morrisoni). *June:* Caddis, Golden Stone, Salmonflies (Pteronarcys californica). *July:* Caddis, Green Drake (Ephemerella grandis), PMD (Ephemerella inermis), Red Quill (Rhithrogena hageni), Yellow Sally (Isoperla). *August:* Caddis, PMD, Tricos (Tricorythodes minutus), Yellow Sally, Baetis, Pale Evening Dun (Epeorus albertae), Tiny Olive Quill (Pseudocloeon futile). *September:* Caddis, Baetis, Trico, Olive Quill, Mahogany Dun (Leptophlebia gravastella). *October:* Olive Quill, Baetis. *May-Sept.:* Snowfly (Capnia). *Nov.-Dec.:* Baetis, Midges.

Equipment to Use
Rods: 3-6 weight, 8-9'.
Line: Floating line to match rod weight.
Leaders: 4x to 6x, 9-11'.
Wading: Chest-high waders, felt-soled boots with studs. Boot-foot neoprenes in winter.

Flies to Use
Dries: November-March, Griffith's Gnat, Midge Emerger #18-22, Adams, Black Midge #20-24. *April-May:* BWO, Elk Hair Caddis, Baetis & Adams Parachute #18-22, Midges #18-20. June: Elk Hair Caddis #16-18, Hemingway Caddis #14-18, Sofa Pillow #4-8, Orange Stimulator #4-10. *July-September:* PMD, Light Cahill, Stalcup's CDC Comparadun, AK's Melon Quill #14-18, Adams Parachute #14-20, Elk Hair Caddis #12-16, Dave's & Schroeder's Hopper #10-14, Red Quill #16, CDC Red Quill #14-16. *Nymphs:* all colors Copper John #14-20, Midge Larva, Kimball's Emerger, WD 40, RS-2 #18-22, Pheasant Tail #16-22, Gold-Ribbed Hare's Ear #12-18, Prince (and Beadhead), Chamois #12-16, Olive Scud (below Williams Fork) #14-16, Kaufman's Dark Stone #4-8, Golden Stone #6-10, Bird's Stone #4-10, Beadhead Barr's Emerger BWO #16-22, Barr's Emerger #16-20, Mueller's Otter Nymph #14-18.

When to Fish
Fish all year. Best hatches June to September. Runoff discoloration May to mid-June. Two miles below confluence can have ice Dec.-Feb. Fish Williams Fork almost all year, April-November best.

Seasons & Limits
Catch and release, flies and lures only from Byer's Canyon Bridge to Troublesome Creek. General regulations above Canyon Bridge.

Nearby Fly Fishing
The Blue and Fraser rivers, Upper Williams Fork, and Willow creeks.

Accommodations & Services
Camping at Lone Buck SWA, Pioneer Park in Hot Sulphur Springs and Williams Fork Reservoir. Motels and other services at Hot Sulphur Springs and Kremmling.

Rating
Year-round fishing, good sized fish and prolific hatches make this part of the Colorado a strong 9.

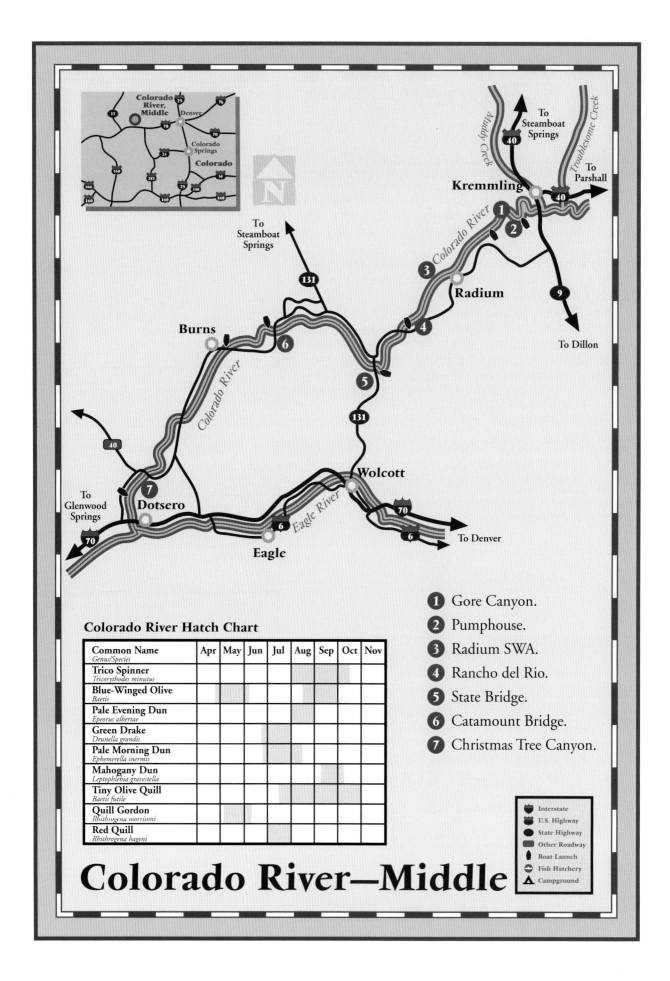

Colorado River—Middle

Colorado River Hatch Chart

Common Name	Apr	May	Jun	Jul	Aug	Sep	Oct	Nov
Trico Spinner *Tricorythodes minutus*								
Blue-Winged Olive *Baetis*								
Pale Evening Dun *Epeorus albertae*								
Green Drake *Drunella grandis*								
Pale Morning Dun *Ephemerella inermis*								
Mahogany Dun *Leptophlebia gravestella*								
Tiny Olive Quill *Baetis futile*								
Quill Gordon *Rhithrogena morrisoni*								
Red Quill *Rhithrogena hageni*								

1. Gore Canyon.
2. Pumphouse.
3. Radium SWA.
4. Rancho del Rio.
5. State Bridge.
6. Catamount Bridge.
7. Christmas Tree Canyon.

Legend:
- Interstate
- U.S. Highway
- State Highway
- Other Roadway
- Boat Launch
- Fish Hatchery
- Campground

Colorado River— Middle
Kremmling to Dotsero

Below the town of Kremmling the Colorado cuts through the spectacular Gore Canyon, dropping dramatically some fifty river miles until it meets the Eagle River at Dotsero. It is best to float the lower end of Gore Canyon, as there are seven good drift sections from Pumphouse to Dotsero. This is not easy water to negotiate. I recommend you get a qualified guide if you want to drift the canyon.

If you want seclusion, try the water up in the canyon above Pumphouse, which is often neglected. It's a tough trail and should be considered only by the young at heart. The payoff, however, is pristine water that changes character around every bend.

A drawback to this middle section is during spring runoff when siltation from aptly named Muddy Creek makes the fishing spotty. Wolford Mountain Reservoir and a new dam on this creek have eliminated much of the problem. Also, in June-August lots of rafters take this day trip and add to the crowd.

To get to this section of the Colorado from Highway 9, go two miles south of Kremmling and take Trough Road west. From Interstate 70, exit at Dotsero and take Colorado River Road along the river, or take Highway 131 from Wolcott north to State Bridge.

Gore Canyon on the Colorado River. Photo by Jim Muth.

Types of Fish
Brown and rainbow trout, Colorado River cutbows and whitefish.

Known Hatches
The siltation problem from Muddy Creek reduces hatches on this section.
March-April: Midges (Diptera). *May-June:* Blue-Winged Olive (Baetis) and Caddis. *July-August:* PMD (Ephemerella inermis) Red Quill (Rhithrogena hageni), Caddis. *August-October:* Trico. *September:* Red Quill, Baetis. *October-November:* Baetis, Midges.

Equipment to Use
Rods: 4-7 weight, 8 1/2-9 1/2'.
Reels: Mechanical or palm drag.
Lines: Floating and sink tip for streamer fishing.
Leaders: 1x to 5x, 9'.
Wading: Chest-high breathables and felt-soled boots. Wet wading is possible in August.

Flies to Use
Dries, March-April: Midge, Betts Midge & Stalcup's Midge Emerger, Blue-Winged Olive, Griffith's Gnat #18-22, Baetis Parachute, Adams Parachute, Stalcup's CDC Baetis #18-20. *May-June:* Stimulator #8-10, Royal Wulff #8-12, Elk Hair Caddis #12-14, Baetis, Blue-Winged Olive #18-20. *July-August:* Schroeder's Para-Hopper, Dave's Hopper, Royal Wulff, H&L Variant #8-12, Humpy, Irresistible, Lime Trude #8-14, PMD #14-18. *September-October:* Baetis Parachute #18-20, Red Quill #14-16, Wulff, Adams Parachute, Stimulator, Hoppers #10-12. *Nymphs & Streamers:* Gold-Ribbed & Beadhead Hare's Ear, Prince (also Beadhead) #10-16, Pheasant Tail #14-18, Copper John #14-20, Red Squirrel Tail #12-14, Beadhead Barr's Emerger BWO #16-22, Rubber Leg Stone #6-8, Woolly Bugger, Flashabugger, Matuka # 2-6, Blackburn's Sculpin #1-2, Improved Girdle Bug #4-8, Trico Spinners #18-22.

When to Fish
Generally, fish anytime before or after spring runoff. July-October offers the best fly fishing, and cloudy days bring out the better fish. The middle part of the Colorado River, in slow sections, freezes over December to early March.

Seasons & Limits
Fish year-round. Consult Colorado fishing regulations or a nearby fly shop.

Nearby Fly Fishing
The Blue, Eagle and Roaring Fork rivers. Piney, Rock, Derby, Troublesome, Muddy and Sweetwater creeks.

Accommodations & Services
Camping is available along the river at spots designated for boaters. Open camping is permitted on BLM land. Motels, restaurants and other services are available in Kremmling and the Vail area.

Rating
With over fifty miles of scenic river and relatively light fishing pressure, this section of the Colorado is a 7.

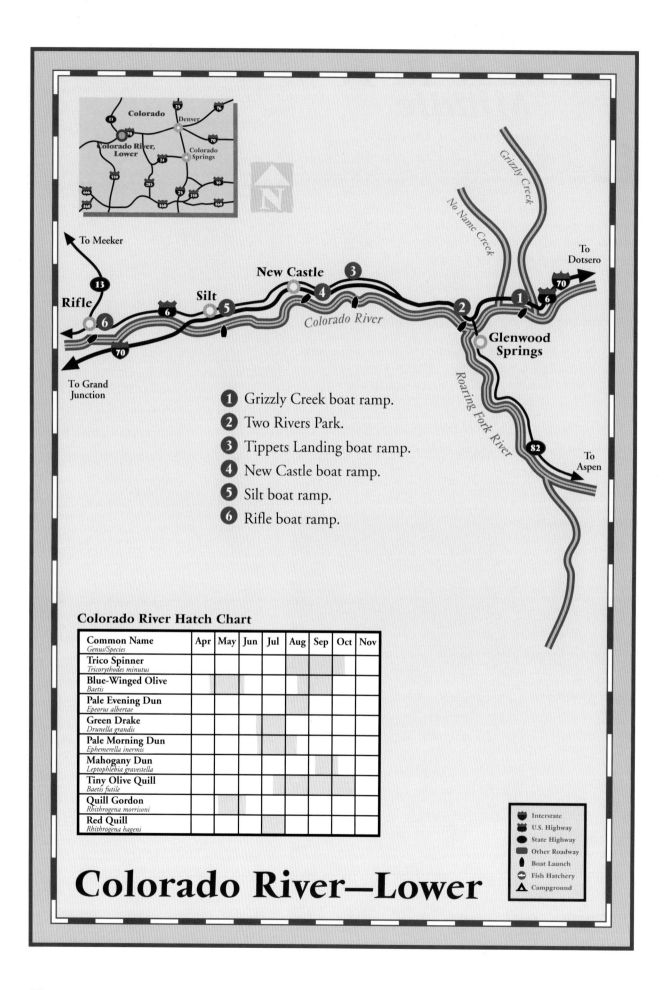

Colorado River—Lower

Colorado

Denver

Colorado Springs

Colorado River, Lower

To Meeker

Rifle

Silt

New Castle

Colorado River

Glenwood Springs

To Dotsero

To Grand Junction

To Aspen

Grizzly Creek

No Name Creek

Roaring Fork River

1. Grizzly Creek boat ramp.
2. Two Rivers Park.
3. Tippets Landing boat ramp.
4. New Castle boat ramp.
5. Silt boat ramp.
6. Rifle boat ramp.

Colorado River Hatch Chart

Common Name Genus/Species	Apr	May	Jun	Jul	Aug	Sep	Oct	Nov
Trico Spinner Tricorythodes minutus								
Blue-Winged Olive Baetis								
Pale Evening Dun Epeorus albertae								
Green Drake Drunella grandis								
Pale Morning Dun Ephemerella inermis								
Mahogany Dun Leptophlebia gravestella								
Tiny Olive Quill Baetis futile								
Quill Gordon Rhithrogena morrisoni								
Red Quill Rhithrogena hageni								

Interstate
U.S. Highway
State Highway
Other Roadway
Boat Launch
Fish Hatchery
Campground

Colorado River— Lower

Grizzly Creek to Rifle

The trout in this section of the Colorado receive relatively light pressure, especially considering the fine fly fishing opportunities available. Floating is really the best way to cover this water, which may, in part, account for the relatively low numbers of fly fishers.

This section, below the Shoshone power station at Grizzly Creek through Glenwood Springs to the Roaring Fork, is a fairly large river. From here downstream, however, the Colorado becomes quite a large river, at least by Colorado standards. Good fly fishing and about six good float trips are available from here all the way to Rifle. There is also adequate access from along Interstate 70 and farther downriver along Highway 6.

To reach this stretch of the Colorado, take Interstate 70 west (about 2 1/2 hours from Denver). At Glenwood Canyon take the Grizzly Creek exit.

Floating this section of the Colorado is the best way to cover the water. Photo by Brian O'Keefe.

Types of Fish
Rainbow and brown trout, Colorado River cutbows, whitefish, some brookies and cutthroats.

Known Hatches
There aren't many hatches on this stretch, but you'll see some of these throughout the year.
April-May and October-November: Mayflies, Baetis. *June-July:* PMD (Ephemerella infrequens), Red Quill (Rhithrogena hageni). *August-September:* Caddis. *May-September:* Sporadic Salmonflies (Pteronarcys californica). *June:* Yellow Sally (Isoperla). *July-August:* Midges (Diptera). *August-September:* Tricos.

Equipment to Use
Rods: 5-7 weight, 8 1/2 - 9 1/2'.
Reels: Mechanical or palm drag.
Line: Floating and sink tip to match rod weight.
Leaders: 1x to 5x, 8-10'.
Wading: Chest-high breathables with felt-soled wading boots. Wet wading only during the heat of summer. McKenzie-style drift boats are a fine way to float, especially with experienced boaters.

Flies to Use
Dries, November-March: Midge, Griffith's Gnat, Biot Emerger, Betts Midge Emerger #18-22.
April-May: Baetis Parachute, Blue-Winged Olive #18-20, Elk Hair Caddis #16-18, Lime Trude #14-16.
June-August: Elk Hair Caddis #14-16, Lime Trude, Rio Grande King Trude #12-14, Royal Wulff #10-14, Stimulators #8-14, Humpies #10-14, Irresistible, Dave's Hopper, Schroeder's Para-Hopper #10-12. *September-October:* Ants #12-14, Hoppers #8-12, Wulff, Humpies #10-12, Baetis #18-20, Adult & Trico Spinner #18-22.
Nymphs: Pheasant Tail, Hare's Ear, Prince #12-16 the same in Beadhead, all colors Copper John #14-20, Woolly Bugger, Flashabugger, Zonker #2-6, Sculpin #2/0-2, Midge Larva #18-20, Beadhead Barr's Emerger BWO #16-22.

When to Fish
Fish year-round, but the best time of year is August to October. The discoloration from runoff peaks by mid-June.

Seasons & Limits
From Troublesome Creek downstream to Rifle Creek, bag and possession limit for trout is two fish. Fifty yards upstream and downstream of Canyon, Grizzly and No Name Creek, fishing prohibited from March 15 to May 15.

Nearby Fly Fishing
Try the Eagle, Roaring Fork, Crystal and Fryingpan rivers plus Grizzly, Derby and Canyon creeks.

Accommodations & Services
There aren't many designated campgrounds along the river. There are many motels, hotels and cabins in Glenwood Springs. The towns of Silt and Rifle also have motels. All other services are readily available in all three towns.

Rating
Relatively light fishing pressure with good results make this section of the Colorado a strong 7.

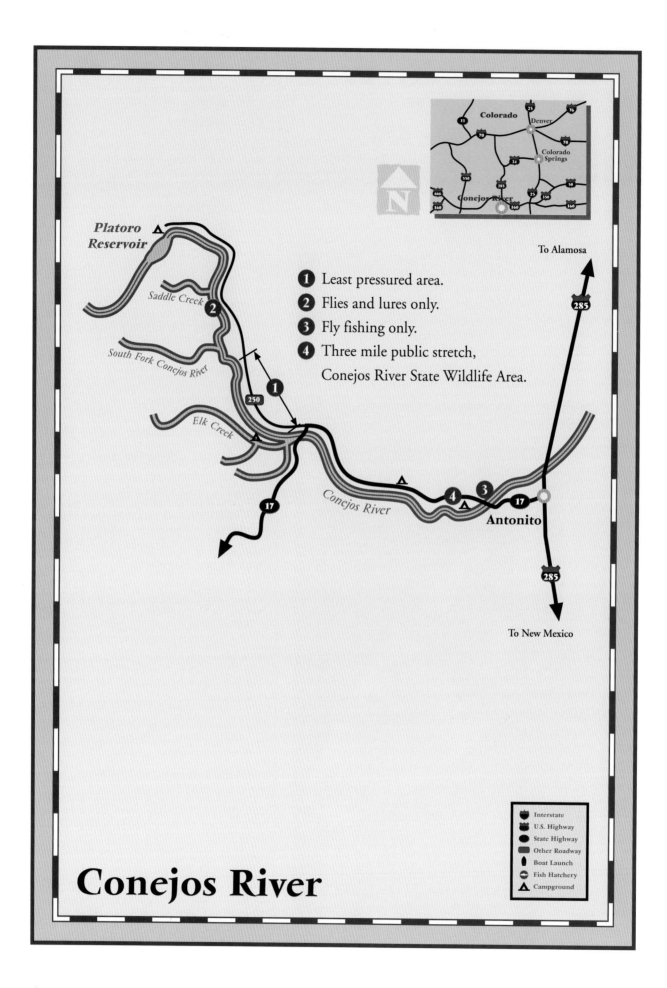

Colorado

Denver

Colorado
Springs

Conejos River

**Platoro
Reservoir**

Saddle Creek

South Fork Conejos River

Elk Creek

Conejos River

To Alamosa

285

250

17

17

Antonito

285

To New Mexico

1 Least pressured area.

2 Flies and lures only.

3 Fly fishing only.

4 Three mile public stretch,
Conejos River State Wildlife Area.

Interstate
U.S. Highway
State Highway
Other Roadway
Boat Launch
Fish Hatchery
Campground

Conejos River

Conejos River

In August 1973, longtime friend Chris Owen and I were on the loose and on a two-week excursion to fly fish as many Colorado rivers as possible. Once we fished the Conejos, it was hard to try others. The river just would not let us leave. I still recall fondly those early, uncrowded years on the Conejos. I urge anyone passing through the southern part of Colorado to stay in the pine-covered mountains for a few days and fall in love with the beautiful canyon setting and river.

This gem of a trout stream may not yield the numbers and large-sized fish of years gone by, but considering the scenery and over sixty miles of fishable water, it's well worth a fly fishing trip. Plus, recent habitat improvements and designation of many sections as Wild Trout Waters have improved the fishery. One can wade most of the river, which averages about sixty feet wide, and there are miles and miles of public access.

To find the Conejos River, head to the south central city of Alamosa and then take Highway 285 to the town of Antonito (if coming from New Mexico also take 285). In Antonito, turn west on Highway 17 just south of town. The river parallels this road for thirty-five miles until you get to a right turn at Forest Road 250. Take 250, as it parallels the river some twenty-five miles all the way to Platoro Reservoir.

Look for Golden Stoneflies June – early July along the Conejos. Photo by Brian O'Keefe.

Types of Fish
Brown, rainbow and cutthroat trout, brookies and some northern pike.

Known Hatches
The Conejos is a typical Colorado trout stream. Water can be high and dirty most of June. *March-May:* Baetis. *May-August:* Caddis. *June-early July:* Golden Stone (Acroneuria pacifica). *Late June-July:* Pale Morning Dun (Ephemerella inermis & infrequens). *September-October:* Baetis.

Equipment to Use
Rods: 3-5 weight, 8-9'.
Reels: Palm or mechanical drag.
Line: Floating to match rod weight.
Leaders: 4x to 6x, 8-9'.
Wading: Chest-high breathable waders and felt-soled boots.

Flies to Use
Dries: Elk Hair Caddis, King's River Caddis, Adams, Humpy, Wulff, Irresistible #14-18, Baetis Parachute, Blue-Winged Olive #16-20, Hoppers, Beetles, Ants #14-16. *Streamers:* Bugger, Zonker, Matuka, Muddler #2-6. *Nymphs:* Hare's Ear (also Flashback), Pheasant Tail #14-18, Prince (also Beadhead) #12-16, Copper John #14-20, Muskrat #14-16, Bird's Stone #8-12, Beadhead Barr's Emerger BWO #16-22, Midge Larva #18-22, Brassies #18-20.

When to Fish
The river opens and is fishable in April but heavy snows can make getting around difficult. The best fly fishing is after runoff: late June through September. The best dry fly fishing is mid-July through mid-September. After Labor Day weekend, fishing pressure clears and the changing colors of aspen trees add to the reward.

Seasons & Limits
Check Colorado regulations, as rules are complex and can change from time to time. Fish the general season. All public use, except fly fishing, is prohibited on the Bear Creek subdivision, HEBO Corporation and Douglas properties from Aspen Glade Campground upstream approximately four miles to Menkhaven Ranch. Fishing by artificial flies only. The bag, possession and size limit for trout is two fish, 16" in length or longer. The same rules apply from the Saddle Creek Bridge downstream to and including the Hamilton property (confluence of Conejos and South Fork of the Conejos). Menkhaven Ranch downstream to the Aspen Glade Campground is Wild Trout Water where general Colorado fishing regulations apply unless posted otherwise.

Nearby Fly Fishing
The Rio Grande and San Juan rivers. Fly Fishing at Platoro Reservoir can be inconsistent.

Accommodations & Services
There are campgrounds along Highway 17 and Forest Road 250. The town of Antonito has gas, motels and groceries. Boat rental at Platoro Reservoir.

Rating
Varied water types and a pristine setting in a lightly-traveled part of Colorado make the Conejos a 7.

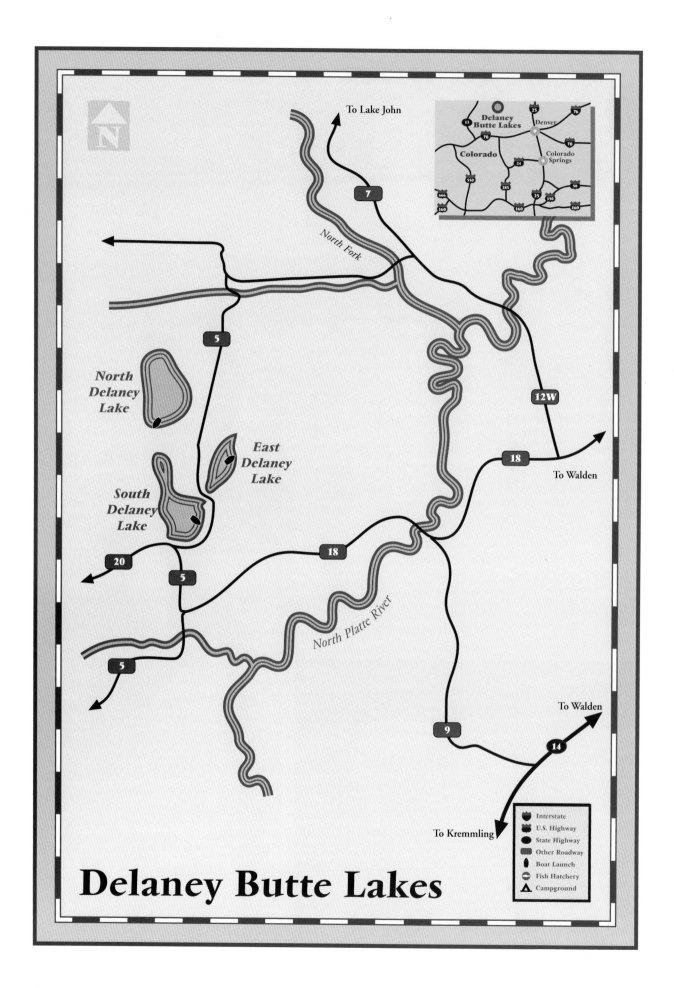

To Lake John

North Fork

Delaney Butte Lakes

Denver

Colorado

Colorado Springs

7

5

North Delaney Lake

East Delaney Lake

South Delaney Lake

12W

18

To Walden

20

5

18

North Platte River

5

9

To Walden

14

To Kremmling

Interstate
U.S. Highway
State Highway
Other Roadway
Boat Launch
Fish Hatchery
Campground

Delaney Butte Lakes

Delaney Butte Lakes

Head to the north central section of the state to the area known as North Park for some great Gold Medal lake fly fishing. About ten miles west of the town of Walden you'll find a group of lakes called Delaney Butte Lakes State Wildlife Area.

The surroundings, at 8–10,000 foot elevation, are stark. These lakes are anything but barren when it comes to food for trout, however. Food sources include scuds, damsels, large sedges, Callibaetis and some forage fish.

The information here is based on experience with the North Lake, a Gold Medal fishery, and can be, in general, applied to the other lakes in this area. In fact, don't pass up East Delaney, South Delaney and to the north, Lake John. They're good fisheries too.

As for North Lake, this is a brown trout fishery only. They average 14-22" with larger fish always possible. Very little if any natural spawning takes place. Nymphing and streamer fishing seem to be the most successful, but some sporadic dry fly fishing is available if you keep a sharp eye. Drop-offs and weed flats are the best places to concentrate your fly fishing.

To reach the lakes from the Fort Collins area, travel west about 100 miles on Highway 14 to Walden. From Walden go 5.5 miles west on 12 W Road to County Road 18, then 4.5 miles west to County Road 5, then one mile north.

Types of Fish
Brown trout.

Known Hatches
June-August: Damselflies.
June-August: Callibaetis Mayflies.
July: Caddis.

Equipment to Use
Rods: 5-6 weight, 9-10'.
Reels: Mechanical or disc drag.
Line: Floating and sink tip to match rod weight.
Leaders: 2x to 5x, 9-10'.
Wading: Not much area to wade, a float tube or boat is best.

Flies to Use
Dries: Olive & Grey Sedges #6-8, Dry Damsels #6-12, Adams Parachutes, Callibaetis patterns #16-18, assorted Midges #18-22. *Nymphs:* Olive & Grey Scuds #10-14, Black AP #12-16, Brown & Olive Damselfly #8-12, Zug Bug #12-18, all colors Copper John #14-20, Beadhead Barr's Emerger BWO #16-22. *Streamers:* Various Zonkers, Buggers & Matukas #2-4.

When To Fish
Early to mid-May, right after ice-out, the fishing is good throughout the day. During summer, early or late in the day is best.

Seasons & Limits
Open year-round, fishing by artificial flies and lures only. The bag and possession limit for trout is two fish. Brown trout between 14–20" must be returned to the water immediately.

Nearby Fly Fishing
North Fork of the Platte River, Canadian River, Michigan and Grizzly creeks, plus Lake John and Walden Reservoir.

Accommodations & Services
Camping is available in the Delaney Butte Lakes State Wildlife Area. There are a limited number of motel rooms and services in Walden.

Rating
Winter fish kills can be a problem here. If there have been a few years between kills, these lakes are a strong 8.

An Olive Damselfly Nymph (top) is a good summertime choice for Delaney Butte area lakes. Photo by Brian O'Keefe.

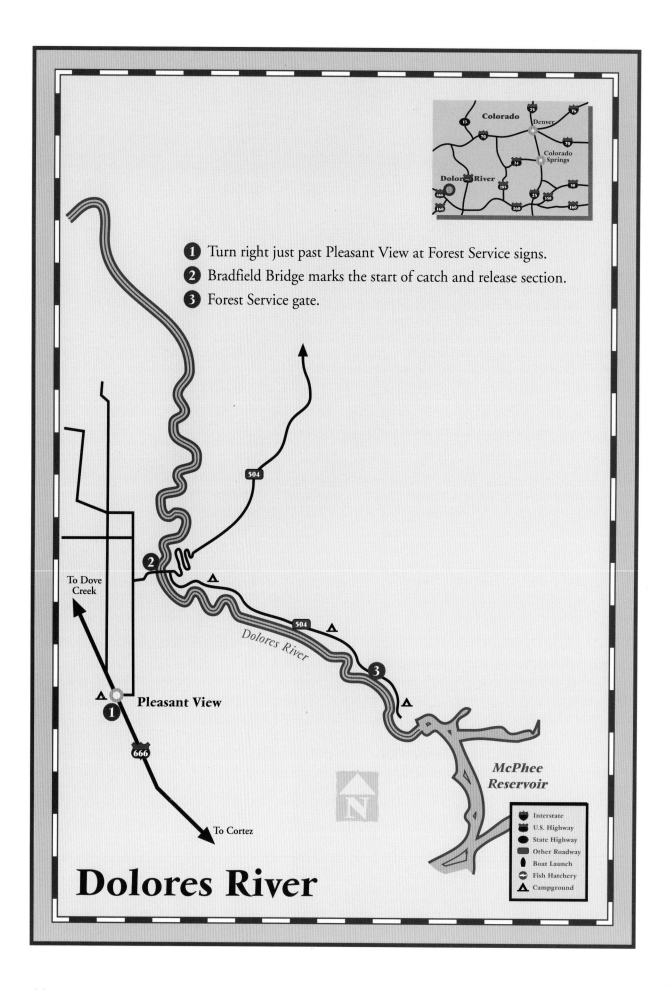

1 Turn right just past Pleasant View at Forest Service signs.
2 Bradfield Bridge marks the start of catch and release section.
3 Forest Service gate.

Colorado
Denver
Colorado Springs
Dolores River

504

To Dove Creek

Dolores River

504

McPhee Reservoir

Pleasant View

666

To Cortez

N

Interstate
U.S. Highway
State Highway
Other Roadway
Boat Launch
Fish Hatchery
Campground

Dolores River

Dolores River

Anglers say they leave a part of themselves on the river every time they experience the out-of-the-way Dolores. Located in the far southwest corner of the state, this is one of Colorado's best fisheries, with horseshoe bends and a canyon section that is truly unique.

The river starts high on Lizard Head Pass (10,222 feet) and runs southwest with Highway 145 to the town of Dolores and McPhee Reservoir. The stretch is a typical high alpine freestone stream featuring rainbow trout, two campgrounds and lots of private land and water.

At McPhee Reservoir the river hooks to the northwest. The section below the earthen dam is pristine tailwater for eleven miles to Bradford Bridge. This is the stretch most people refer to as the Dolores. It's catch and release and there are plenty of access roads, campgrounds and picnic areas thanks to the state of Colorado and the U.S. Forest Service. To reach this section of the Dolores, drive north from Cortez on Highway 666. Look for Road CC, or a right turn just past Pleasant View, and follow the signs to the river.

Fly fishing the Dolores, especially during low water, can be very technical. Matching the hatch of insects shown can be key. Fly patterns for tailwaters and spring creeks seem to work best.

Look for Caddis hatches all year on the Dolores, but mostly from June through August. Photo by Brian O'Keefe.

Types of Fish
Rainbow, brown and cutthroat trout.

Known Hatches
April: Stoneflies (Willowflies, Acroneuria pacifica). *Mid-June to August:* Various Caddis (hatches year-round). *Mid-June to October:* Blue-Winged Olives (Baetis). *Late-September to November:* Midges (Diptera, hatches year-round). *October-November:* Tiny Olive Quill (Pseudocloeon anoka). *Mid-July to September:* Pale Morning Dun (Ephemerella infrequens).

Equipment to Use
Rods: 3-5 weight, 8-9'.
Reels: Disc or pawl that have very low drag settings.
Line: Floating to match rod weight.
Leaders: 5x to 8x, 9-16'.
Wading: You'll walk a lot along the Dolores. Take lightweight equipment like hippers. Wet wade in the summer.

Flies to Use
Dries: Comparadun, Thorax patterns #16-22, Low-water Caddis patterns #14-20, Elk Hair Caddis #14-18, Midge adult patterns #20-28, Stonefly #10. *Nymphs & Streamers:* Mayfly #14-22, Barr's Tan Emerger #18-22, Caddis Larva & Pupa, all colors Copper John #14-20, Midge Larva & Pupa #18-24, Beadhead Barr's Emerger BWO #16-22, Stonefly #6-14, Muddler #4-8, Sculpin #2-4.

When to Fish
The best fishing begins after runoff, around the middle of June in most years. The river fishes well with good insect activity into late November. The first six miles of river is closed to auto traffic December 1 to April 1, providing elk a protected winter range.

Seasons & Limits
The entire river is open year-round. From McPhee dam downstream to the Bradford Bridge (eleven miles) artificial flies and lures only. All trout must be returned to the water immediately.

Nearby Fly Fishing
McPhee Reservoir, West Fork of the Dolores River, and McJunkin, Barlow, Lizard Head, Slate, Coke Oven, Snow Spur, Bear and Coal creeks.

Accommodations & Services
One of the charms of the Dolores is that it's close to nowhere. Many anglers stay in Durango and drive two hours each way. There are adequate facilities in Cortez and Dolores. Summer camping on the river is excellent, with quality facilities available.

Rating
With seclusion and scenery, great hatches and even better fly fishing, the Dolores easily rates a 9.

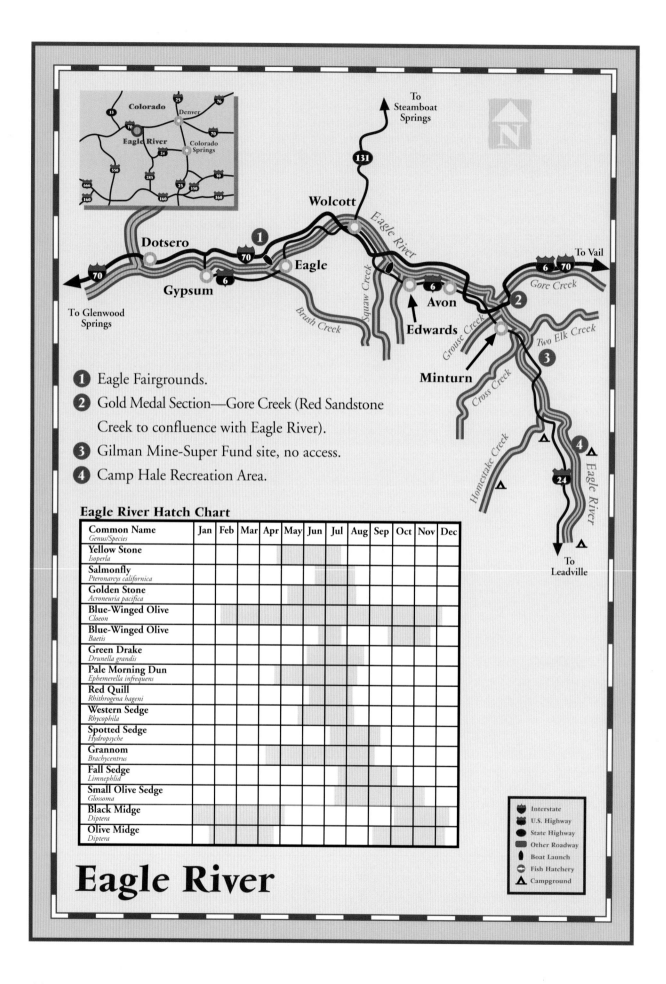

To Steamboat Springs

131

Wolcott

Eagle River

To Vail

6 70

Gore Creek

Colorado

Denver

Eagle River

Colorado Springs

Dotsero

70

Eagle

Gypsum

6

Squaw Creek

Avon

6

2

Edwards

Grouse Creek

Two Elk Creek

Minturn

3

To Glenwood Springs

Brush Creek

Cross Creek

To Vail

Homestake Creek

24

Eagle River

4

To Leadville

N

1 Eagle Fairgrounds.

2 Gold Medal Section—Gore Creek (Red Sandstone Creek to confluence with Eagle River).

3 Gilman Mine-Super Fund site, no access.

4 Camp Hale Recreation Area.

Eagle River Hatch Chart

Common Name *Genus/Species*	Jan	Feb	Mar	Apr	May	Jun	Jul	Aug	Sep	Oct	Nov	Dec
Yellow Stone *Isoperla*												
Salmonfly *Pteronarcys californica*												
Golden Stone *Acroneuria pacifica*												
Blue-Winged Olive *Cloeon*												
Blue-Winged Olive *Baetis*												
Green Drake *Drunella grandis*												
Pale Morning Dun *Ephemerella infrequens*												
Red Quill *Rhithrogena hageni*												
Western Sedge *Rhycophila*												
Spotted Sedge *Hydropsyche*												
Grannom *Brachycentrus*												
Fall Sedge *Limnephlid*												
Small Olive Sedge *Glossoma*												
Black Midge *Diptera*												
Olive Midge *Diptera*												

Interstate
U.S. Highway
State Highway
Other Roadway
Boat Launch
Fish Hatchery
Campground

Eagle River

Eagle River

The Eagle is a beautiful river (especially in the fall) that many locals are proud to call their home water. The wild trout are colorful and strong, averaging fifteen inches with many in the 18-21 inch range. For many years, the Eagle has been overshadowed by the Colorado, Roaring Fork and Fryingpan rivers. As a result, one is often fly fishing alone here—a goal of many.

If there's a meat-and-potatoes kind of trout stream in Colorado, it's the Eagle, and for many reasons. Much of the seventy-plus-mile river is open to public fishing. One can wade the Eagle during much of its prime season. It contains all the classic types of challenging fly fishing water. The hatches are many, varied and predictable, and Eagle River trout, while not terribly selective, are not pushovers.

The medium-sized, freestone stream averages 45-50 feet across, with flows between 275-350 cfs. Runoff typically begins mid-May, with the river becoming wadeable again by mid- to late July.

Floating the Eagle is quite popular during a special period after runoff when the water clears. This is usually from early June until the river drops so low it can't be floated. Be careful, the Eagle is a rocky, technical river with a number of tight, class IV rapids during high water. Hire a knowledgeable outfitter if you plan to float. Plus, there is a lot of private water, so watch for signs.

To reach the Eagle, drive west on I-70 (from Denver) to Highway 24, west of Vail. This is also called Highway 6, which parallels the river all the way to Dotsero. To get to the upper sections go south on Highways 6 and 24, just west of Vail.

Fishing a run on the Eagle River. Photo by Jim Muth.

Types of Fish
Reproducing rainbow and brown with brook and cutthroat in the higher reaches.

Known Hatches
Stoneflies, Salmonflies, Blue-Winged Olive, Pale Morning Dun, Green Drake, Caddis, Sedge, Midges. Please refer to the hatch chart.

Equipment to Use
Rods: 4-6 weight, 8-9'.
Reels: Palm or mechanical drag.
Line: Floating to match rod weight.
Leaders: 4x to 7x, 9-10'.
Wading: It's slippery. During high water use chest-high waders with felt or studded felt-soled boots. Hippers can be used in late summer and fall. A wading staff is helpful.

Flies to Use
Dries: Yellow Bucktail Caddis #10-12, Orange Bucktail Caddis #8-10, Blue-Winged Olives #18-20, Adams Parachute, Adams #14-20, Light Cahill & Cahill Adams #14-16, Green Drake, Royal Wulff, Michigan Killer #12-14, Elk Hair Caddis #12-16 (various colors). *Nymphs:* Yellow Stone, Twenty Incher, Green Drake #12-14, Black & Yellow Stone, Halfback #8-10, Pheasant Tail #12-20, all colors Copper John #14-20, Light Cahill, Prince #14-16, Olive Partridge Soft-Hackle, LaFontaine's Brown & Green Pupae #14-18, Olive Biot Caddis Larva, Bristle-Back #12-14, Hare's Ear #10-12, Brown Hackle Peacock #14-20. *Emerger & Wets:* Red Quill Poly-Wing, Adams Parachute, Light Cahill #14-16, Green Drake Poly-Wing #12-14, Caddis Emerger #12-18, Beadhead Barr's Emerger BWO #16-22.

When to Fish
From mid-July to mid-August most of the significant summer hatches are in progress and fly fishing can be best. From early December until late February the Eagle is mostly iced-over and open waters are few and far between. This starts to change in late February. Nymphing is quite good throughout the spring and fish rise to Midges and small Mayflies.

Seasons & Limits
All public and posted areas (with permission) are open year-round. The bag and daily possession limit is two trout. There are no restrictions on tackle, but it is best to check current Colorado fishing regulations.

Nearby Fly Fishing
The Colorado, Roaring Fork, Piney and Blue rivers. Homestake and Gore creeks.

Accommodations & Services
There are numerous hotels, motels and condominiums throughout the valley from Vail to Gypsum and plenty of campgrounds along the river. Tackle and guide services are also available in the area.

Rating
For ease of access, good solid hatches and above average trout, the Eagle easily rates an 8.

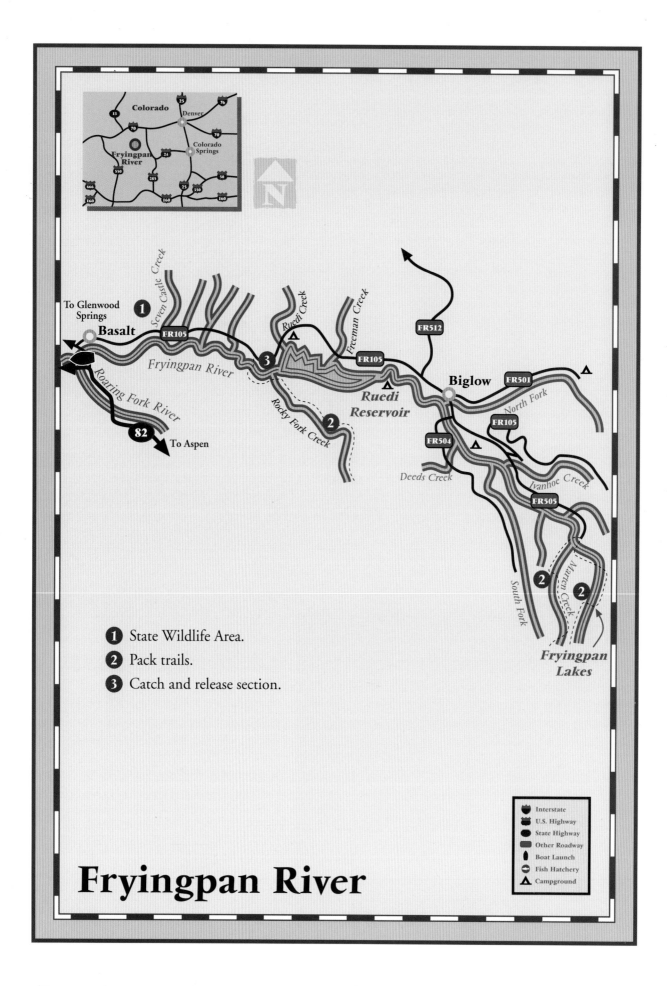

Colorado

Denver

Colorado
Springs

Fryingpan
River

To Glenwood
Springs

Basalt

1

Seven Castle Creek

FR105

Fryingpan River

Roaring Fork River

82

To Aspen

Ruedi Creek

3

Rocky Fork Creek

2

Freeman Creek

FR105

*Ruedi
Reservoir*

Biglow

FR512

FR501

FR105

North Fork

FR504

Deeds Creek

Ivanhoe Creek

FR505

South Fork

Marten Creek

2

2

*Fryingpan
Lakes*

1 State Wildlife Area.

2 Pack trails.

3 Catch and release section.

Interstate
U.S. Highway
State Highway
Other Roadway
Boat Launch
Fish Hatchery
Campground

Fryingpan River

Fryingpan River

The Fryingpan River is among the best known and loved trout streams in the nation. It is a must for anyone fly fishing in Colorado. The river is managed to maximize recreation and to grow large, wild trout.

The upper Fryingpan, above Ruedi Reservoir, is a small, intimate high-country stream. Along with its major tributaries, it offers fine summer and fall fishing for feisty trout. Their willingness to take a fly and their sheer numbers make up for their lack of size.

The fourteen miles of water between Ruedi and the confluence with the Roaring Fork in Basalt is a Gold Medal Fishery in every sense. Incredible insect hatches and Mysis shrimp (from the outlet of Ruedi Dam) give the trout plenty of food to grow to trophy proportions. Although heavily fished during certain times of the year, this section of "the Pan" remains a favorite for those who seek the challenge of large and selective fish. Look for private sections that require permission to pass.

To find the Fryingpan from Interstate 70, drive southeast from Glenwood Springs on Highway 82 to the town of Basalt. Look for Fryingpan River Road, which parallels the river. Access is readily available.

A busy day on the 'Pan. Photo by David Banks.

Types of Fish
Brook, brown, cutthroat and rainbow, with browns and rainbows most common.

Known Hatches
Year-round: Midges (most important December-March). *Mid-June to mid-October:* Caddis.
Mid-July to September: Mayflies, Green Drake (Ephemerella grandis), Pale Morning Dun (Ephemerella inermis & infrequens).
March to May & September to November: Blue-Winged Olive (Baetis).

Equipment to Use
Rods: 3-5 weight, 8-9'.
Reels: Mechanical or palm drag.
Lines: Floating to match rod weight.
Leaders: Tapered from 5x to 7x, 9-12'.
Waders: A tailrace fishery, the Pan is cold year-round. Breathable waders with felt-soled boots work best.

Flies to Use
Given the multitude of hatches, try to match what's on or in the water.
Dries: Green Drake #10-12, Pale Morning Dun, Blue Dun, numerous Caddis #14-18, Red Quill #16-18, Blue-Winged Olive #18-22, Midges #22. During Non-hatch Periods: Midge Larva & Pheasant Tail #18-22, Beadhead Barr's Emerger BWO #16-22, all colors Copper John #14-20, Prince & Buckskin nymphs, Western Coachman #14-18 are among the favorites.

When to Fish
The Fryingpan is a great open year-round fishery, so fly fish here whenever you can.

Seasons & Limits
Current regulations allow the harvest of two brown trout under 14". All other fish must be returned to the water immediately. These rules can change; always check Colorado regulations or at a fly shop.

Nearby Fly Fishing
Try the Roaring Fork and Colorado rivers plus smaller waters such as Crystal River and Maroon, Castle and Snowmass creeks.

Accommodations & Services
There are campgrounds around Ruedi Reservoir. All major services can be found in or near Basalt and farther down the road in Carbondale, Glenwood Springs and Aspen.

Rating
The intimate nature of the stream, abundance of trout, the opportunity of a lifetime for a trophy and the fact that you can sight-fish to many trout in a day makes The 'Pan a unique jewel among the many fine waters in Colorado, and a true 10.

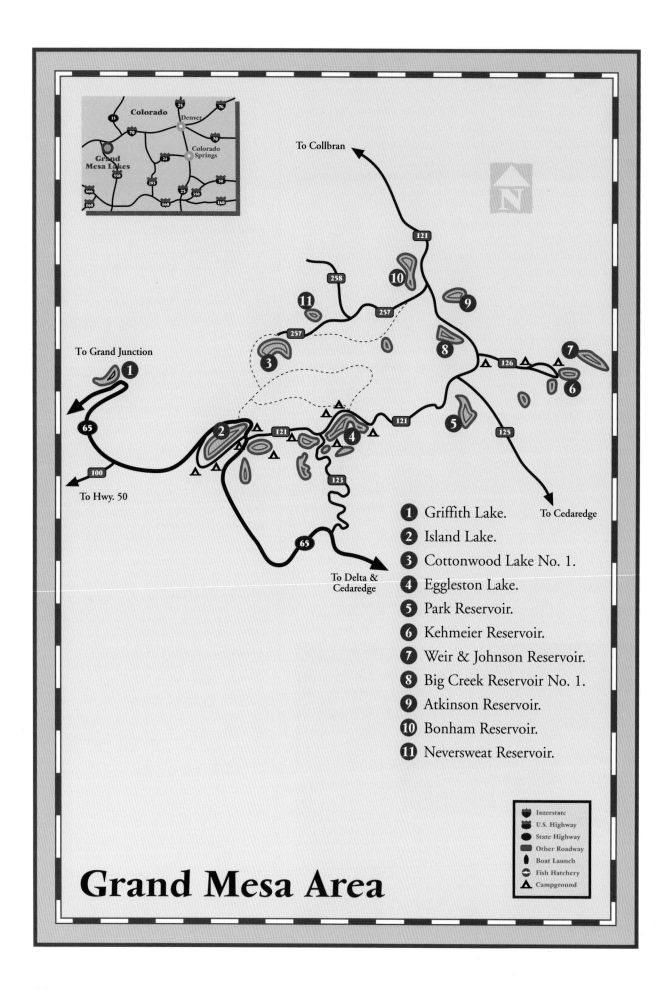

Colorado

To Collbran

121

258

257

To Grand Junction

257

To Hwy. 50

To Delta &
Cedaredge

To Cedaredge

1 Griffith Lake.

2 Island Lake.

3 Cottonwood Lake No. 1.

4 Eggleston Lake.

5 Park Reservoir.

6 Kehmeier Reservoir.

7 Weir & Johnson Reservoir.

8 Big Creek Reservoir No. 1.

9 Atkinson Reservoir.

10 Bonham Reservoir.

11 Neversweat Reservoir.

Interstate
U.S. Highway
State Highway
Other Roadway
Boat Launch
Fish Hatchery
Campground

Grand Mesa Area

Grand Mesa Area

Grand Mesa, as this huge flat-top mountain area is called, rises to over 10,000 feet in elevation and is covered with forest and meadows and has over 200 lakes, creeks and streams. This area has long been a favorite for backpackers, campers and anglers. If you're looking to wet a fly line in a dense grouping of various types of waters amid beautiful scenery at high elevation, then Grand Mesa is your spot. But do come prepared for mosquitoes.

Fishing pressure can be heavy on the easily reached lakes and creeks, but for those willing to stray off the beaten track, fly fishing can be excellent. The Colorado Division of Wildlife stocks most of the lakes, but many also hold wild trout populations. Wildlife such as deer, bear and elk are abundant and the terrain varies from semi-arid desert in the lowlands to lush pine and fir forest, aspen groves, meadows, bogs and rocky outcroppings on the mesa. Fly fishing and a visit to this unique and often forgotten part of the great Colorado outdoors can be outstanding.

The waters of the Grand Mesa area are some forty miles east of Grand Junction. Most take Interstate 70 approximately eighteen miles east of Grand Junction to Highway 65. This connects with Highway 92 from the south, not far from Delta.

Types of Fish
Rainbow, cutthroat and brown trout, brookies and splake (brookie/lake trout cross).

Known Hatches
Most of the lakes have Midge hatches throughout the summer as well as Mayfly (Callibaetis) and Damselfly hatches. The streams and creeks have sporadic and insignificant Caddis and Mayfly hatches.

Equipment to Use
Rods: 2-6 weight, 7-9 1/2'.
Reels: Palm or mechanical drag.
Line: Floating, sink tip, and sinking to meet lake depths.
Leaders: 3x to 6x, 7-9'.
Wading: Generally, hip boots work on most of the streams. Float tubing is popular and effective on the lakes. Lake waters are cold, so use chest-high waders while tubing.

Flies to Use
Dries: Thorax Callibaetis, Adams & Adams Parachute #16, Mosquito #12-18, Damsel #6-10, Ants, Beetle #12-14, Hopper #8-12, Wulff, Humpy #14-18. *Nymphs:* Zug Bug, Pheasant Tail, Hare's Ear, all colors Copper John #14-20, Damsel #6-10, Shrimp #12-18, Beadhead Barr's Emerger BWO #16-22, Midge Biot #18-22.
Streamers: Woolly Bugger #2-10, Leech #4-6, Marabou Muddler #4-8.

When to Fish
This area generally gets heavy winter snows, so most prime fly fishing doesn't start until June. The best times are July through August. September can also be good when the crowds have dwindled, but certain waters (especially lakes) can be low due to irrigation demands for nearby orchards. Check with local officials and fly shops for water levels.

Seasons & Limits
There are various regulations for the many different types of waters in this area. There isn't room here to mention them all. Refer to the Colorado Fishing Season Information and Wildlife Property Directory for specific regulations and seasons or inquire at nearby fly shops.

Nearby Fly Fishing
Colorado River, Gunnison River.

Accommodations & Services
There are several campgrounds and a couple of lodges on the mesa. The nearest motels are about fourteen miles away in the towns of Cedaredge to the south and Mesa to the northwest. Limited supplies (food and gas) are available on the mesa. Boats can be rented at some lakes.

Rating
For the unique combination of high-altitude lakes and streams, this area rates a 9.

A float tube is a fun way to hook up with trout in the lakes of the Grand Mesa area. Dress warmly. Photo by Brian O'Keefe.

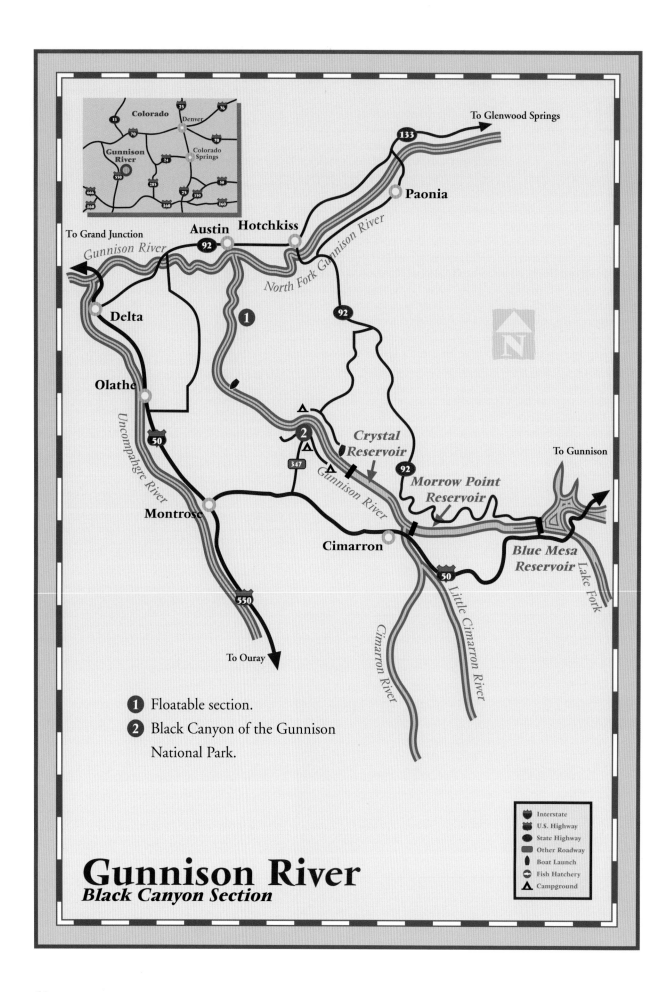

To Glenwood Springs

Colorado
Denver
Colorado Springs
Gunnison River

133
Paonia
To Grand Junction
Austin Hotchkiss
92
Gunnison River
North Fork Gunnison River
Delta
1
92
Olathe
Uncompahgre River
Crystal Reservoir
50
2
To Gunnison
347
Gunnison River
92
Morrow Point Reservoir
Montrose
Cimarron
50
Blue Mesa Reservoir
Lake Fork
550
Cimarron River
Little Cimarron River
To Ouray

1 Floatable section.
2 Black Canyon of the Gunnison National Park.

Gunnison River
Black Canyon Section

Interstate
U.S. Highway
State Highway
Other Roadway
Boat Launch
Fish Hatchery
Campground

Gunnison River
Black Canyon Section

Awesome. Spectacular. Fantastic. These are just a few of the adjectives that describe this section of the Gunnison, where fly fishing is as good as the scenery.

These fifty-three miles are famous for leaping rainbows, stonefly hatches, and very difficult access. Below Blue Mesa Reservoir where the Black Canyon begins, two dams create some great tailwater-type fly fishing. One has to get there by foot, and some places on the trail have a drop of almost 3,000 feet. Be careful hiking in, contact local authorities, be in good physical condition, and plan ahead. Better yet (and highly recommended), contact one of the better outfitters who float the lower section of the canyon. They know the area, and the descent is much easier in this section. Don't consider floating this dangerous canyon without full knowledge of the river. Enough said.

The most spectacular stretch of water, for fly fishing and scenery, runs through the Black Canyon National Park area.

To drive to this river section, head east from Montrose on Highway 50 about ten miles. The park entrance is on County Road 347. Alternatively, travel west on Highway 50 from Gunnison to below Blue Mesa Reservoir. There are enjoyable trails on either side of the canyon and from Peach Valley Road, south of the town of Austin. Use local maps and information from an area fly shop to find other access.

The painted wall, chasm view, Black Canyon of the Gunnison National Park, North Rim. Photo by Quang-Tuan Luong, Terra Galleria Photography.

Types of Fish
Rainbow, brown, and cutbows.

Known Hatches
April-May & September-October: Mayflies, BWO.
May-September: Various Caddis.
June-early July: Stoneflies (Pteronarcys californica).
June-July: PMD (Ephemerella infrequens), Caddis.

Equipment to Use
Rods: 4-7 weight, 9'.
Reels: Mechanical or palm drag.
Line: Floating and sink tip to match rod weight.
Leaders: 1x to 5x, 8-10'.
Wading: Generally cold water. Carry in lightweight waders and felt-soled boots.

Flies to Use
Dries, April-May: BWO, Midges & Adams #18-22, some Caddis in May. *June-July:* Sofa Pillow #2-6, Stimulator #4-8, Elk Hair Caddis #8-16, Schroeder's Para-Hopper, Dave's Hopper, Trude #8-12, Humpies #12-14. *August:* Elk Hair Caddis #12-16, Trude #12-14, Wulff #14-16, Schroeder's Para-Hopper #8-12, Ants & Beetles #12. *September:* Schroeder's Parachute Hopper, Dave's Hopper, Joe's Hopper #8-10, Blue-Winged Olive #20-22. *Nymphs:* Kaufman's Stone #4-6, Prince #4-16, Hare's Ear #6-16, Pheasant Tail #8-18, Bird's Stone, Twenty Incher #4-8, Beadhead Prince, Beadhead Hare's Ear #8-14, Tellico Nymph, Barr's Net Building Caddis #12-14, all colors Copper John #14-20, Beadhead Barr's Emerger BWO #16-22, Caddis Larva #10-14, Woolly Bugger #2-6.

When to Fish
The best dry fly fishing is June during the stonefly hatch. It's hard to be there at just the right time. June water can also be discolored and high during heavy snow years. Check at a fly shop for water flows: best below 1,500 cfs. Nymphing is good all year.

Seasons & Limits
Most of this river is Gold Medal and Wild Trout water and open year-round. From the upstream boundary of the Black Canyon of the Gunnison National Park to the North Fork of the Gunnison, fish artificial flies and lures only. Release all fish 12-16". Check current Colorado fishing regulations for bag, possession, and size limits.

Nearby Fly Fishing
The North Fork of the Gunnison, Lake Fork, Cimarron, Uncompahgre and San Miguel rivers and Cebolla and Curecanti creeks.

Accommodations & Services
Campgrounds in the national park and one in the canyon at the east portal. Register with the ranger at the park. Motels, hotels, and all major services in Montrose and Delta. Cabins and camping at Pleasure Park (888-782-7542) where they'll also take you up the lower section of the canyon if you are drifting or touring.

Rating
Breathtaking views, superb fly fishing—this section of the Gunnison definitely rates a 10.

High Alpine Lakes

Colorado offers the fly fisher hundreds of fishable lakes that sit near or above the tree line. There are too many to list here. Just take this general information, scan a good map, consult a fly shop and head for the hills. If you're adventurous enough to go off fly fishing via four-wheel, backpack or day hike, you'll be rewarded with beautiful remote lakes and trout that are hungry for a fly. I highly recommend fly fishing Colorado's high alpine lakes.

Over a period of years the Division of Wildlife and the U.S. Forest Service have stocked, from aircraft, nearly all high mountain lakes in Colorado. Most have cutthroat trout, but rainbow and brook trout are also prevalent. A few lakes have golden trout and grayling.

Many of these lakes receive virtually no fishing pressure, so catching can be relatively easy. Crystal clear waters, however, make for selective fish and demand proper presentation.

Pay attention to weather. Although it may be warm and sunny on the valley floor, at 12,000 feet in elevation, colder, winter-type weather persists through June. For this reason most high mountain lakes do not thaw until late June or even July.

As mentioned, it's always a good idea to check with local fly shops for information about lakes you're interested in before attempting an ascent. Local information can help make a high mountain fly fishing trip much easier. Plus, many of the hikes up to the lakes bring you by smaller creeks and streams that are often chock full of hungry brook and cutthroat trout. Most of these waters have never seen an artificial fly, and rewards are realized in short order. A local shop can point you in the right direction.

Above: Rocky Mountain National Park has many beautiful high alpine lakes. Photo by Quang-Tuan Luong, Terra Galleria Photography.
Facing page: Hike in to fly fish Montgomery Reservoir near Alma, with 14,285 foot Mt. Lincoln in the distance. Photo by Jim Muth.

Types of Fish
Generally cutthroat, but rainbow, brook and lake trout can also be found. Some lakes even have golden trout and Arctic grayling.

Known Hatches
Most lakes above the tree line have few major hatches. Midges are the most common insects for these fish. Below the tree line, there's more insect life, especially Damsels, Callibaetis and other Mayflies and Midges.

Equipment to Use
Rods: 4-5 weight, 8-9 1/2'.
Reels: Mechanical or palm drag are fine.
Line: Floating, sink tip, and sinking to match rod weight and depending on lake depth.
Leaders: Usually 4x - 6x, 7-1/2'.
Wading: Generally, because of drop-offs or other bottom conditions, wading is limited at most alpine lakes. Carry in a float tube, fins and waders for best results.

Flies to Use
Dries: Terrestrials like ants, beetles and crickets work well in sizes #8-14. Also Midge dries like Adams, Midge Emergers #18-22. Attractor dries in sizes #18-22 will also produce. *Nymphs:* Hare's Ear, Zug Bug #16-18, Damsel #8-12, Muskrat #14-18, Midge Larva #18-22, Beadhead Barr's Emerger BWO #16-22, all colors Copper John #14-20. *Streamers:* Woolly Bugger, Zonker, Leech #4-8, Marabou Muddler #4-10.

When to Fish
The period right after ice-out, sometimes late June, can be very good, but it's hard to know exactly when the thaw occurs. Always check with a fly shop or Forest Service office in the area you plan to visit (see the back section of this book for a listing). Most lakes freeze again by late September. Dry fly fishing seems to be better early or late in the day when the sun angle and calm water are conducive to hatches and feeding. Also, because of the ever-present chance of afternoon storms and lightning (and virtually no cover), trips early in the day are recommended.

Seasons & Limits
These will vary from lake to lake, so a listing here is impractical. Check Colorado fishing regulations and at fly shops.

Rating
The trip and fishing can be a pleasant change from the crowded tailwaters down below. A rating for lakes at this altitude is not important. The experience is always a 10.

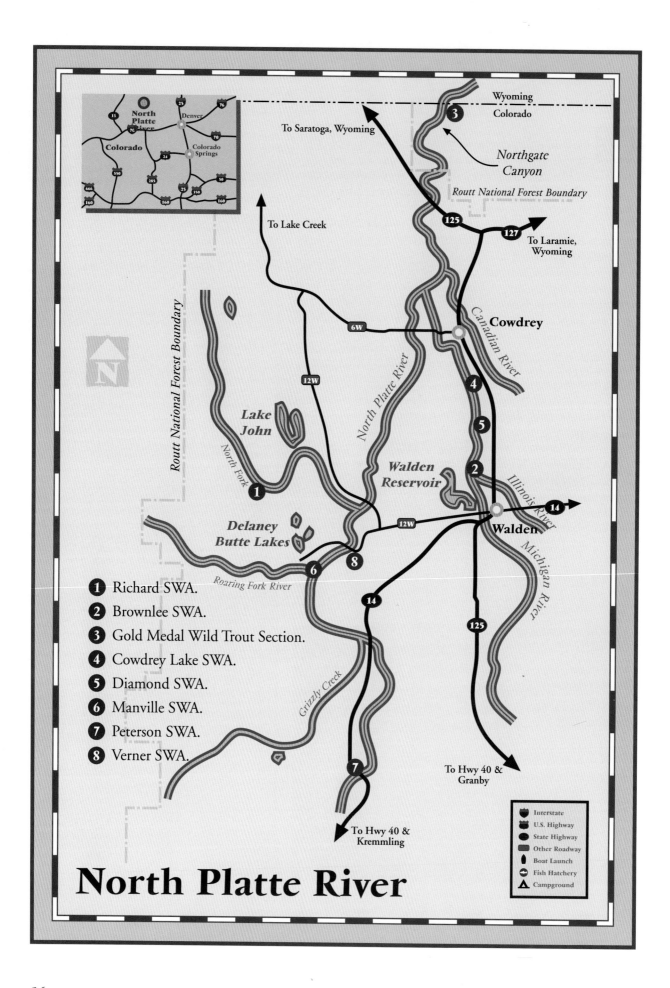

Wyoming
Colorado

To Saratoga, Wyoming

③

Northgate
Canyon

Routt National Forest Boundary

125

127 → To Laramie, Wyoming

To Lake Creek

6W

Cowdrey

Canadian River

④

⑤

12W

Routt National Forest Boundary

North Fork

Lake John

North Platte River

②

Walden Reservoir

Illinois River

Delaney Butte Lakes

12W

14 →

Walden

⑧

125

Michigan River

⑥

Roaring Fork River

① **Richard SWA.**

② **Brownlee SWA.**

③ **Gold Medal Wild Trout Section.**

④ **Cowdrey Lake SWA.**

⑤ **Diamond SWA.**

⑥ **Manville SWA.**

⑦ **Peterson SWA.**

⑧ **Verner SWA.**

14

Grizzly Creek

⑦

To Hwy 40 & Granby

To Hwy 40 & Kremmling

North Platte River

Interstate
U.S. Highway
State Highway
Other Roadway
Boat Launch
Fish Hatchery
Campground

North Platte River
North Fork

The North Platte runs through a vast, grassy basin called North Park. Not surprisingly, this area is similar to South Park, some 150 miles to the southeast, if you need a point of comparison. The water is a meandering, oxbow meadow-type river and is one of the few rivers that flows north and out of Colorado.

The North Platte and tributaries start high and clear in the Mount Zirkel Wilderness. The North Fork of the North Platte also feeds into the North Platte and is a fine fly fishing stream. Both rivers offer many and varied fishing opportunities, as in the South Park area. There are deep pools, riffles and flat water. All fly fishing techniques will take fish on this river.

Access along private properties seems to change yearly. Contact the North Park Ranger District in Walden for current information.

You can have good to mediocre fly fishing on the other tributaries in the area: Grizzly and Norris creeks, and the Canadian, Illinois and Michigan rivers. More important, these waters provide many nutrients, which help the fish in the North Platte grow to about 10-16 inches.

The river changes to narrow, fast-moving water at Northgate Canyon. About midway through the canyon is the Wyoming state line. A Wyoming fishing license is required if fishing farther down the canyon.

To get to the North Platte from the Steamboat Springs area drive east on Highway 40 and north on Highway 14. From the east drive to Granby and take Highway 125 toward Walden.

Typical grassy banks and meandering river in North Park. Photo by Brian O'Keefe.

Types of Fish
Brown and rainbow trout.

Known Hatches
April-May & September-October: Blue-Winged Olives (Baetis).
September-early October: Tricos (Tricorythodes).
June-September: Caddis (various).
July-August: Midge (Diptera) fall & spring, Yellow Sally (Isoperla).

Equipment to Use
Rods: 4-7 weight, 8-9'.
Reels: Palm or mechanical drag.
Line: Floating and sink tip to match rod weight.
Leaders: 3x to 6x, 8-10'.
Waders: Hippers are fine on upper reaches. Use breathable waders with felt-soled boots for the canyon.

Flies to Use
Dries: Adams Parachute #14-18, Foam-Winged Baetis, Midge patterns #18-22, Poly-Winged Adams #16-18, Elk Hair Caddis #14-16.
Terrestrials: Hoppers, Beetles, Ants, #10-16.
Nymphs: Pheasant Tail #16-20, Beadhead Hare's Ear #12-16, Beadhead Barr's Emerger BWO #16-22, Midge & Caddis Larva and Pupa #18-22, all colors Copper John #14-20.
Streamers: Matuka, Bugger, Sculpin, Zonker #2-4.

When to Fish
March and April can be quite good before runoff. Late June to October is the best time.

Seasons & Limits
Fish year-round. Generally, water is frozen December to February. From the southern boundary of the Routt National Forest downstream to the Wyoming state line, it is Gold Medal and Wild Trout water: fish with artificial flies and lures only. The bag and possession limit for trout is two fish. On Brownlee and Verner SWAs, fish with artificial flies and lures only. On North Fork of the North Platte River on the Richard SWA, fish with artificial flies and lures only. Always consult the regulations book.

Nearby Fly Fishing
Delaney Butte Lakes, Lake John and the Colorado River.

Accommodations & Services
Public campgrounds along the river are limited, but there are others within an easy drive. A few motels and limited services are available in Walden. Stock up and gear up before you head out.

Rating
The North Platte and area is a solid 7.

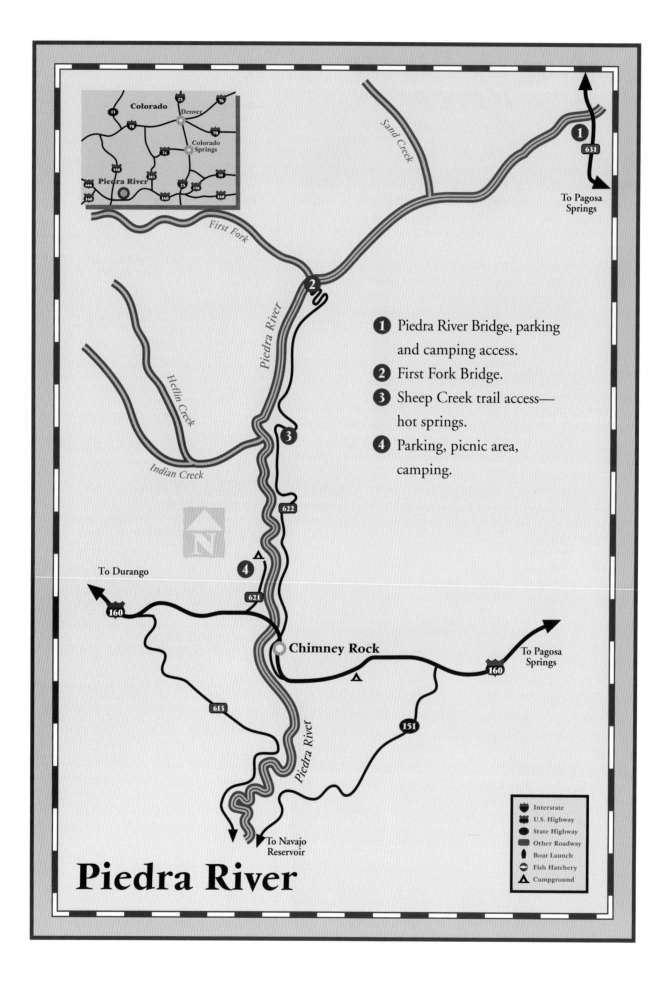

1 Piedra River Bridge, parking and camping access.

2 First Fork Bridge.

3 Sheep Creek trail access— hot springs.

4 Parking, picnic area, camping.

Piedra River

Interstate
U.S. Highway
State Highway
Other Roadway
Boat Launch
Fish Hatchery
Campground

To Pagosa Springs

To Durango

To Navajo Reservoir

To Pagosa Springs

Chimney Rock

Sand Creek

First Fork

Piedra River

Heflin Creek

Indian Creek

631

160

622

621

613

151

160

Piedra River

The Piedra (stone in Spanish) is located about as far south in Colorado as one can go. It flows south out of the San Juan Mountains and joins the San Juan River to form Navajo Lake. It offers some forty miles of exceptionally beautiful wild trout fly fishing with lots of pools, riffles and slow-moving sections. Portions of this thirty-foot-wide freestone stream have been considered for designation and protection as a Wild and Scenic River.

Summer storms and snow runoff have a great influence on the Piedra. It's generally "out" during the very best late spring stonefly activity. In most years the river clears and fishes quite well by mid-June. The clear waters of August run 150-250 cfs. Getting onto the river requires a little guidance.

South of Highway 160 the river is mostly private. There is a short stretch of public access, however, just north of the highway up Forest Road 621 on the west side of the river. With more private property and steep canyons, the next most reasonable access is at Sheep Creek several miles upstream and off County Road 622, or First Fork Road, which parallels the river on the east side of the river. The next access point is at the First Fork Bridge where the road dead-ends roughly 12 miles north of the highway on 622.

To find this section of the Piedra, travel east on Highway 160 from Durango, or west from Pagosa Springs to Chimney Rock. Look for Forest Roads 621 and 622 on either side of the river to head upstream. The other access point is well upstream at the Piedra River Bridge. To find this section, drive west of Pagosa Springs two miles and drive about 12 miles on the Piedra Road 631.

Types of Fish
Brown and rainbow trout, some exceptionally large.

Known Hatches
There are two hatches of real interest to fly fishers.
April-August: Various Caddis.
May: Stoneflies (Acroneuria pacifica).

Equipment to Use
Rods: 4-6 weight, 8 1/2 to 9'.
Reels: Disc or palm drag.
Line: Floating to match rod weight.
Leaders: 3x to 5x, 9'.
Wading: Chest-high breathable waders with felt-soled boots. Lightweights are best in summer heat.

Flies to Use
Dries: Elk Hair Caddis, Humpy, Irresistible, Wulff, Trude #14-18, Hoppers #10-12. *Nymphs & Streamers:* Prince #12-16, all colors Copper John #14-20, Beadhead Barr's Emerger BWO #16-22, Halfback #8-12, Western Coachman #12-14, Hare's Ear (also in Beadhead) #12-16, Bird's Stone, Twenty Incher #6-10, Woolly Bugger #4-6.

When to Fish
The Piedra is a summer to early fall fishery. A large part of the San Juan Mountains drain into the river and area storms can cloud and adversely affect the river (for fly fishing). Fish tributaries immediately after summer rains.

Seasons & Limits
Fly fish year-round. From the Piedra River Bridge on USFS Road 631 (Piedra Road) downstream to the lower boundary of Tres Piedras Ranch (1.5 miles above Highway 160), artificial flies and lures only. Access Road 631 just west of Pagosa Springs. The bag and possession limit for trout is two fish per day.

Nearby Fly Fishing
The Florida, San Juan, East and Middle fork of the Piedra and Animas rivers. Deadman, Williams, Plumtaw and Pagosa creeks.

Accommodations & Services
There is one campground about one mile north of Highway 160 on Forest Road 621. Many anglers travel from nearby Durango or Pagosa Springs, where all major services are available.

Rating
Relatively light pressure on the Piedra, lots of wild trout and the chance for large fish easily make this southern Colorado river an 8.

A large brown is possible from the Piedra. Photo by Brian O'Keefe.

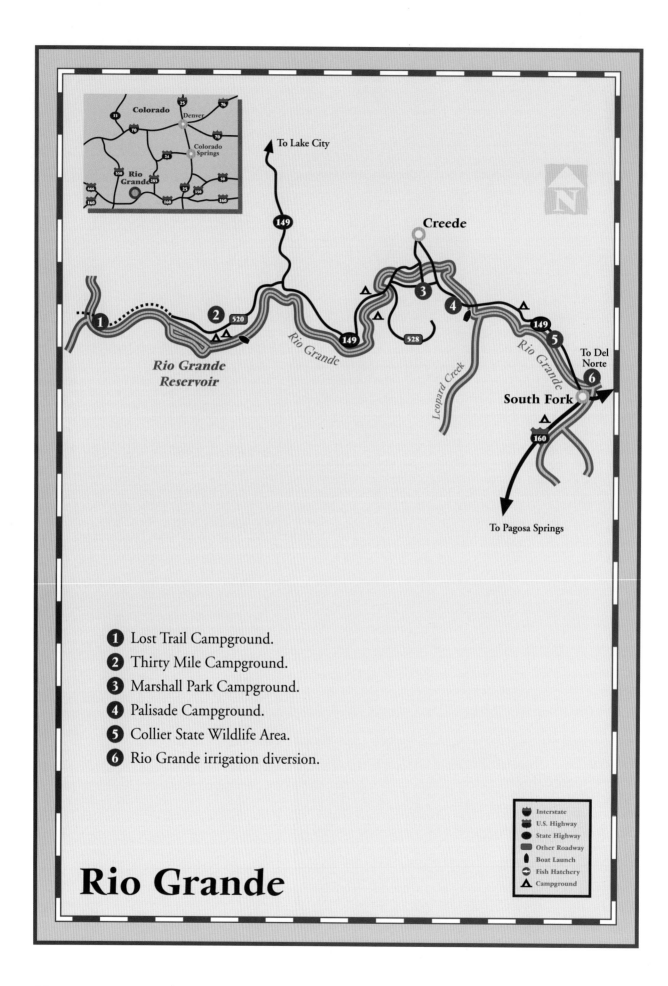

To Lake City

Creede

Rio Grande

Rio Grande Reservoir

Leopard Creek

Rio Grande

To Del Norte

South Fork

To Pagosa Springs

1 Lost Trail Campground.

2 Thirty Mile Campground.

3 Marshall Park Campground.

4 Palisade Campground.

5 Collier State Wildlife Area.

6 Rio Grande irrigation diversion.

Interstate
U.S. Highway
State Highway
Other Roadway
Boat Launch
Fish Hatchery
Campground

Rio Grande

Rio Grande

The Rio Grande (The Big River) and its many tributaries offer a wide range of fishing opportunities, from small creek fishing to the challenge of a larger freestone river. There's an abundance of aquatic insect life in this fine trout fishery, including several species of Mayflies and Caddis and fine populations of Stoneflies.

This famous river begins as a small stream high in the San Juan Mountains, above Rio Grande Reservoir, about twenty-seven miles west of Creede. There are brown, cutthroat and rainbow trout in the reservoir, but fishing can be irregular depending on water levels.

The Colorado portion of the river's trout fishery extends from the headwaters to just west of Del Norte where much of the water is diverted for irrigation. In this seventy-five mile stretch of river there is a mixture of private and public access. The public water is a combination of National Forest, State Wildlife areas and lands leased by the state.

Rio Grande. Photo by Jackson Streit.

Type of Fish
Above Rio Grande Reservoir rainbow, brown, cutthroat and brook trout. Below Rio Grande Reservoir brown trout with some rainbows.

Known Hatches
Mid-June to early July: Salmonflies (Pteronarcys californica), Golden Stone (Acroneuria pacifica), Yellow Stone (Isoperla). *Late June-early July:* Green Drake (Ephemerella grandis), Pale Morning Dun (Ephemerella infrequens). *June-August:* Variety of Caddis. *September-October:* Blue-Winged Olive (Baetis).

Equipment to Use
Rods: 4-6 weight, 8 1/2 to 9'.
Lines: Floating lines to match rod weight.
Leaders: 3x to 6x, 9'.
Wading: In early summer and late fall, use chest-high breathables with felt-soled boots. In warm weather and low water, use hip boots or wade wet.

Flies to Use
Dries: Royal Wulff, Elk Hair Caddis, Stimulator #10-16. *Nymphs:* Prince, Hare's Ear #10-18, Western Coachman #12-16, all colors Copper John #14-20, Beadhead Barr's Emerger BWO #16-22. *Streamers:* Black Woolly Bugger #6-10, Platte River Special, Muddler Minnow, Girdle Bug #4-8. *Mid-June to July Dries:* Sofa Pillow #4-6, Golden Stone #6-12, H&L Variant #10-16, Elk Hair Caddis #12-18. *Nymphs:* Beadhead Caddis Larva #12-16, Bitch Creek, Black Stone, Halfback #4-8, Green Drake Emerger #10-12. *August Dries:* Royal Wulff #14-18, Hoppers #8-14, Madam X #8-12, Muddler Minnow (dry) #4-10, Royal Trude #12-16. *Nymphs:* Pheasant Tail, Hare's Ear #12-18. *September-October Dries:* Comparadun #18-20, Adams #16-20. *Nymphs:* Pheasant Tail #16-20, Flashback Nymph #18-20, Brassie #18-22. *Streamers:* Black Woolly Bugger #6-10, Spruce Fly #4-10. *Winter Dries:* Adams #18-22, Comparadun #10-16. *Nymphs:* Midge Pupa #18-24, Prince #14-18.

When to Fish
Above Rio Grande Reservoir the end of June into September is best. In mid-June the river below Rio Grande Reservoir will usually drop and clear, providing the best dry fly action through mid-July. The section below the town of South Fork fishes best with lower water. July to September is best.

Seasons & Limits
There is no closed season for trout. Special restrictions apply in several areas. Consult the Colorado Division of Wildlife regulation book.

Nearby Fly Fishing
Rio Grande and Beaver Creek reservoirs, Goose and Heart lakes, Park, Embargo, West Bellows and North Clear creeks and South Fork of the Rio Grande.

Accommodations & Services
Camping is available within the Rio Grande National Forest at a number of designated campgrounds. The communities of South Fork and Creede provide adequate hotels, food and groceries.

Rating
The Rio Grande is a solid fishery with an abundance of fish in the 12-16" range, with larger fish scattered throughout. Overall, a 7.

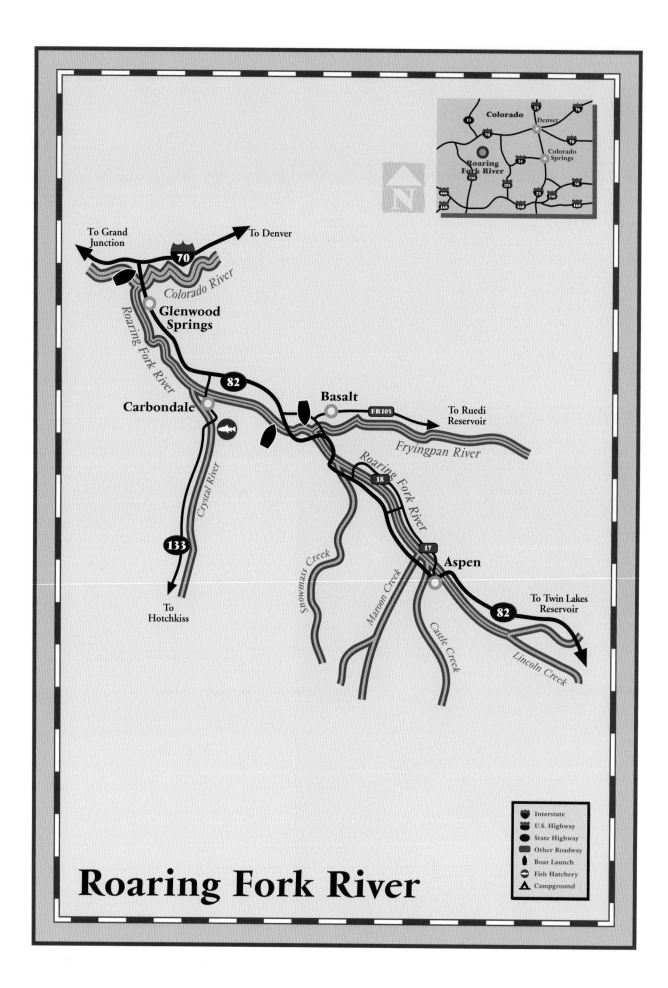

Roaring Fork River

Legend:
- Interstate
- U.S. Highway
- State Highway
- Other Roadway
- Boat Launch
- Fish Hatchery
- Campground

Roaring Fork River

The Roaring Fork may be the best relatively unknown river in the nation. From alpine origins high on the slopes near Independence Pass to the confluence with the mighty Colorado River in Glenwood Springs, the Fork is a study in delightful contrasts. Sixty river miles change from meandering high meadow stream to full-sized, brawling western freestone river suitable for McKenzie River drift boats (watch for rocks!). It also varies from small pocketwater to large runs and pools that may require hours to cover properly. The Fork is also among the finest winter fisheries in Colorado. Many visit the area to combine skiing at nearby Aspen with fly fishing.

The Roaring Fork has not achieved the status and ranking it deserves. Perhaps attention goes to its world-famous neighbor, the Fryingpan. In any event, the Fork, with forty miles of Gold Medal Water, holds trout, some up to eight pounds, throughout its entire length.

To get to the Roaring Fork take I-70 to Highway 82 and go toward Aspen. Highway 82 from Glenwood Springs runs southeast along the river to Independence Pass. One can also get to the river from Buena Vista or Leadville from the east by taking Highway 24 to Twin Lakes Reservoir. Go west to get to the twisty pass, which, at 12,095 feet in elevation, closes in the winter due to snow.

A drift boat is a comfortable way to float the Roaring Fork. Photo by Brian O'Keefe.

Types of Fish
Primarily rainbow, brown and whitefish.

Known Hatches
When you see any of these, match them: large, dark Stoneflies or smaller Golden Stone, Green Drakes, Pale Morning Duns and Baetis Mayflies. Blizzards of Caddis are legendary on the Fork.
Year-round: Midges. *Late April-September:* Caddis. *Mid-June to mid-July:* Mayflies, Green Drake (Ephemerella grandis), PMD (Ephemerella inermis). *March-April & September-October:* Blue-Winged Olive (Baetis). *Late May to early June:* Stoneflies, Dark Giant Stone (Pteronarcys californica). *June to mid-September:* Golden Stone (Acroneuria pacifica).

Equipment to Use
Rods: 4-6 weight, 8 1/2-9'.
Reels: Palm or mechanical drag.
Line: Floating or sink tip to match rod weight.
Leaders: 7x for small dries, tapered to 3x for streamer fishing from boats, 7 1/2-9'.
Wading: The bottom of the Fork is like walking on greased bowling balls. Chest waders and good felt-soled boots with cleats and/or a wading staff. In summer, some wet wading is possible.

Flies to Use
Attractors: Wulff, Humpy, H&L Variants, and Irresistible #10-16. *Summer:* Lime, Pink, and Rio Grande King Trude #12-14. *Nymphs:* Prince #8-16 (also in Beadhead) is the best all-around, all-season nymph here, also try all colors Copper John #14-20, Beadhead Barr's Emerger BWO #16-22.

When to Fish
The Roaring Fork fishes well all year except during the brief runoff period. Most years this is from mid-May to mid-June.

Seasons & Limits
Open year-round; bag limits vary depending on the section of river. From McFarlane Creek downstream to the Upper Woody Creek Bridge it's fly only. Return fish to the water immediately. Upper Woody Creek Bridge to the Colorado River, artificial flies and lures only. Bag, possession and size limit for trout is two fish 16" or longer. These rules can change. Always check Colorado regulations or at a fly shop.

Nearby Fly Fishing
The Fryingpan and Colorado rivers should not be missed. Smaller waters include Crystal River, Snowmass Creek, Lincoln Creek, Maroon Creek and Castle Creek.

Accommodations & Services
Camping spaces are scarce along most of the river. There are numerous motels and hotels from Glenwood Springs to Aspen. Basalt and Carbondale are good bases if fishing the Fryingpan and the Roaring Fork. All services are available in Glenwood Springs, Basalt, Carbondale, and Aspen.

Rating
This river meets the desires of most any fly fisher and rates a 9.5.

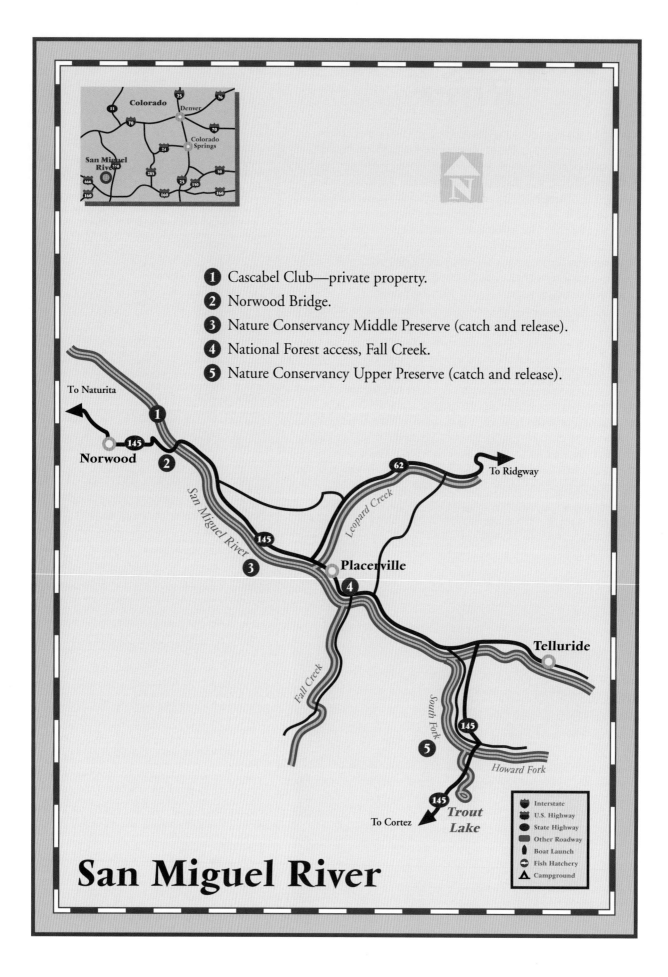

1 Cascabel Club—private property.
2 Norwood Bridge.
3 Nature Conservancy Middle Preserve (catch and release).
4 National Forest access, Fall Creek.
5 Nature Conservancy Upper Preserve (catch and release).

To Naturita

Norwood 145

San Miguel River

To Ridgway

62 Leopard Creek

Placerville

Telluride

Fall Creek

South Fork

145

Howard Fork

Trout Lake

To Cortez

Interstate
U.S. Highway
State Highway
Other Roadway
Boat Launch
Fish Hatchery
Campground

San Miguel River

Colorado
Denver
Colorado Springs
San Miguel River

San Miguel River

This free flowing river runs west-southwest from headwaters above Telluride high in the San Juan Mountains. It is the largest tributary of the Dolores River.

Set in a narrow, steep red rock canyon, the river gradient drops about fifty feet per mile. This makes for some challenging wading. There are fifty miles of good fly fishing water, including the South Fork, that are mostly natural and undeveloped settings. Over 90 percent of the river and its major feeder creeks are accessible and public water. County Road 145 is handy and runs alongside the river.

Another noteworthy point about the San Miguel from a fly fishing perspective is the unsophisticated fish. Successful tactics here can be basic, using nymphs or dries. Here is an excellent tactic for San Miguel fly fishing. Nymphs are a mainstay, especially in off-colored water and in the cold of spring or fall. Trout do not often key on an emergence or hatch and feed on the surface infrequently. Despite this, dry flies and simple attractors consistently draw fish to the surface. Fish a dry fly with a nymph dropper in shallow, swift pocketwater and seams. A longer rod, well-doped large attractor and lightly weighted, medium-sized nymph, two or more feet below the dry, is the ticket. Drift both flies well and you'll catch as many on the dry as the nymph. Use short line casts, outrigger reach and aggressive wading.

The San Miguel is primarily a Caddis river. Look underwater for these types of case caddis. Photo by Brian O'Keefe.

Types of Fish
Brook trout in the upper river and creeks and, in the main section, some reproducing cutthroat, and brown, rainbow and hybrid cutbows. There are also stocked fingerling browns and rainbows.

Known Hatches
In general, the San Miguel is a Caddis river. *May-June:* Caddis (Brachycentrus). *June-September:* Caddis (various). *March-April:* Stoneflies, Snowflies (Capnia). *March-May:* Some Midges, Snowflies (small Stonefly). *June:* Dark Giant Stone (Pteronarcys californica). *Mid-June to mid-July:* Golden Stone (Acroneuria pacifica). *Summer-Fall:* Mayflies, some Baetis (Ephemerella & Rhithrogena).

Equipment to Use
Rods: 4-6 weight, 8-9' or longer.
Reels: Mechanical or palm drag.
Line: Floating to match rod weight.
Leaders: Generally 5x, 7 1/2-8 1/2'.
Wading: A slippery, irregular river bottom with swift water. Chest-high breathable waders with felt-soled boots or cleats. Wet wading is possible on warm, sunny summer days.

Flies to Use
Dries, March-May: Griffith's Gnat, Adams, Grizzly and various other Midge patterns, Trailing Shuck Midge Emerger #18-22. *June:* Water is generally high and dirty. After cold spring storms, water clears and there are Caddis and Stoneflies. Try Elk Hair Caddis #14-18 (all colors) Orange & Yellow Stimulator #8-16, Trude #12-16. *July-September:* Caddis, Trude & Stimulator plus Royal Wulff #12-16, Yellow & Red Humpy #12-14 Hoppers #8-12. *October-November:* Some fall Baetis #18-22.
Nymphs: Prince #10-14, Gold-Ribbed Hare's Ear, Pheasant Tail #14-16, Beadhead Barr's Emerger BWO #16-22, all colors Copper John #14-20, Bitch Creek #6-10, Woolly Bugger #4-8, Sculpin #2/0-2.

When to Fish
The San Miguel fishes quite well March to early May before runoff. The most popular season is when flows drop below 300 cfs, which can be from mid-June to mid-July into November.

Seasons & Limits
As of this writing, the San Miguel is open to fishing year-round and has no special regulations, but it's wise to first check the regulations booklet or at a fly shop.

Nearby Fly Fishing
Fall and Leopard creeks.

Accommodations & Services
Motels, hotels, lodges and gas, restaurants and groceries are in Telluride or the Ridgway/Ouray area. It's mostly day-use parking along the river with very limited camping. Note the BLM designated "Area of Critical Environmental Concern."

Rating
Plenty of access, lots of good-sized fish and generally fair weather make the San Miguel a solid 7.

1. Family Hole and Ice Box: Dry flies.

2. Floating Rock and Steel Riffles: Nymphs.

3. Meat Hole: Nymphs and dries.

4. Emerald Pool: Nice flat, dry flies.

5. Jamboree Pool: Nymphs, deeper water.

6. Iron Springs: Deeper water.

7. Cow's Crossing: Dries and nymphs.

8. Head Cow's Crossing: Sight fishing.

9. Blitz Pool: Dry flies.

10. Blitz Riffle: Good nymphing.

11. Rainbow Pool: Dry flies and nymphs.

12. Rocky Road: Pocketwater, good nymphing.

13. Cleo's Camp, Indicator Pool, Sneak-up Rock, and Pog Hole: Good nymphing.

14. Camel Rock: Good dry fly action.

15. Cat's Crossing: Narrow and deep, good winter holding water.

16. Gaging station: Walk bridge, narrow and deep.

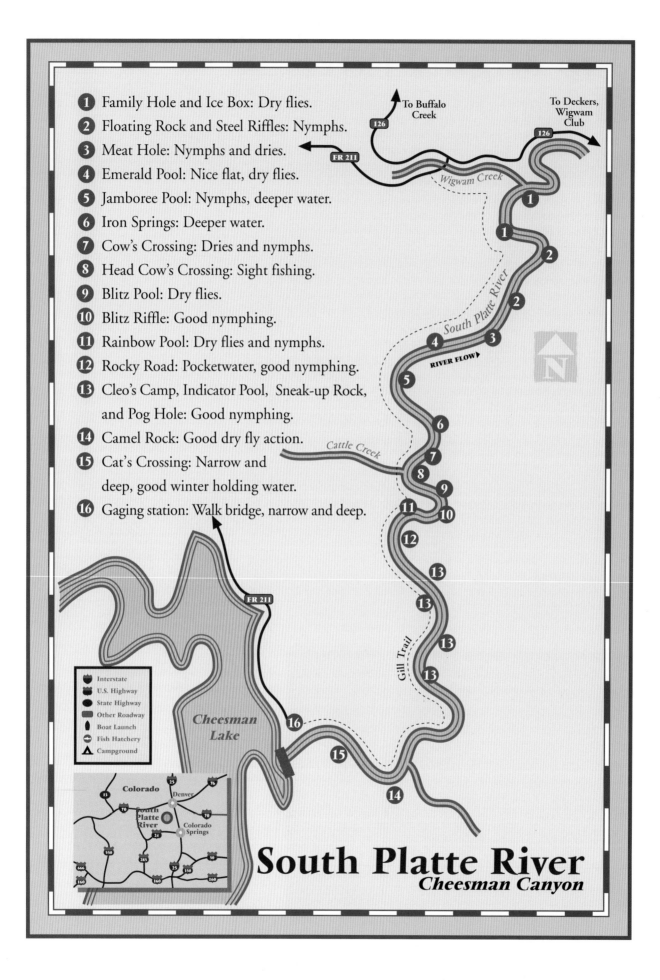

To Buffalo Creek

To Deckers, Wigwam Club

126

126

FR 211

Wigwam Creek

South Platte River

RIVER FLOW ▶

N

Cattle Creek

Gill Trail

FR 211

Interstate
U.S. Highway
State Highway
Other Roadway
Boat Launch
Fish Hatchery
Campground

Cheesman Lake

Colorado
Denver
South Platte River
Colorado Springs

South Platte River
Cheesman Canyon

South Platte River

Cheesman Canyon

The South Platte River, downstream from Cheesman Reservoir, is a world-class fishery offering some of the finest tailwater fly fishing in the state, if not the country. The river below the dam has crystal-clear water and wild rainbow and brown trout. They are eager yet selective. The river survived the huge forest fires that roared through the area in the summer of 2002.

A short hike into the boulder-filled canyon takes one into a wilderness setting rarely found just an hour outside a major metropolitan city such as Denver. The geography is postcard-perfect, and as many visitors say, the fishing is indeed a bonus.

This section of the South Platte usually holds approximately 5,200 trout per mile that average 15". Due to the clear, cold water and heavy fishing pressure, fly selection and presentation are key. Though at times difficult, this section can also produce days that fly fishers dream about. I strongly urge you to see and fly fish this very special place in Colorado.

From the Denver area, drive west on Highway 285 to the town of Pine Junction. Turn south and take Pine Valley Road approximately twenty miles to the well-used parking areas and access just above the private Wigwam Club. Take the Gill Trail into the canyon. You can also drive to Cheesman Reservoir, hike around and down into the upper portion of the canyon. This path is more difficult, especially the return, and you should check at a local fly shop before you consider this route. Access was closed to the public in early 2003.

Lots of rock hopping in this narrow channel of the South Platte in the Cheesman Canyon section. Photo by Lucas Galli.

Types of Fish
Naturally reproducing rainbow, brown and cutbow trout.

Known Hatches
Year-round: Midges (Diptera), most abundant in winter. *March-May & September-November:* BWO (Baetis). *June-July:* PMD (Ephemerella inermis & infrequens). *Mid-June to early July:* Stoneflies (Acroneuria pacifica). *May-September:* Caddis (various). *August-September:* Tricos.

Equipment to Use
Rods: 3-5 weight, 8-9'.
Reels: Disc drag preferred.
Line: Floating to match rod weight.
Leaders: 5x to 7x, 9-14'.
Wading: Water is quite cold for wet wading. In low water, hippers are OK. Use breathable waders and felt-soled boots most of the year.

Flies to Use
January-February: Midges of all kinds, Biot, Griffith's Gnat, Stalcup's Midge Emerger #20-24, Stalcup's Film-Winged Midge #18-24, Betts Midge Emerger #20-26. *March-April:* Previous Midges, Comparadun, Baetis Parachute & Stalcup's CDC Comparadun #18-22. *May:* Baetis #18-22, above Midges, small Caddis. *June:* Stimulators #8-10, Pale Morning Dun & PMD Emergers #18-22, Stalcup's CDC Comparadun, Pink Cahill #18, AK's Melon Quill, Elk Hair Caddis #16-18, Caddis #14-18. *July:* To June selection add Hoppers, Beetles & Ants #14-20, Stones are gone by mid-July. *August-September:* Trico Emergers, Duns & Spinners #20-24, Terrestrials #14-20. *October-December:* Midge #18-24, Still Caddis, Baetis #14-18. *Nymphs:* Pheasant Tail #16-24, Miracle, RS-2, Biot Midge, various colors, Brassies-all colors, Tan San Juan Worms, Olive & Tan WD-40 #18-24, Beadhead Barr's Emerger BWO #16-22, Buckskin, and all colors Copper John #14-20, Black, Brown, Cream, Red & Olive Midge Larva & Pupa #18-26, Orange & Olive Scud #14-18.

When to Fish
Fish whenever you can. Spring water flows best 150 and 250 cfs; flows above 500 cfs make fly fishing difficult.

Seasons & Limits
Open year-round. This is Wild Trout and Gold Medal water: artificial flies and lures only, all fish must be returned to the water immediately.

Nearby Fly Fishing
Nothing within 1 1/2-hour drive.

Accommodations & Services
Camping in the canyon and designated forest campgrounds. A few cabins for rent in Deckers and gas, a restaurant, fly shop and general store.

Rating
If the fish were not so tough, an easy 10. Combine proximity to Denver, big fish, consistent hatches and outrageous scenery for a solid 9.

1. Wigwam Club.
2. Good nymphing, dry flies, bigger fish.
3. Mark's Run: Good nymphing.
4. Diver Hole: Big fish, deep hole.
5. Good for nymphs and dries.
6. Midge Pool: Excellent dry fly water.
7. Good for nymphs and dries.
8. Good nymphing.
9. Bridge Pool: Good for dries and nymphs.
10. Cabin Hole: Deep run, good nymphing.
11. Second Bridge Run: Excellent.
12. Assortment of pocketwater and runs, fishes well.
13. Trumbull Bridge: Great dry fly fishing.
14. Peacock Hole: Good nymphing.
15. Beaver Hut: Great dry fly action.
16. Sway Bar Ranch.

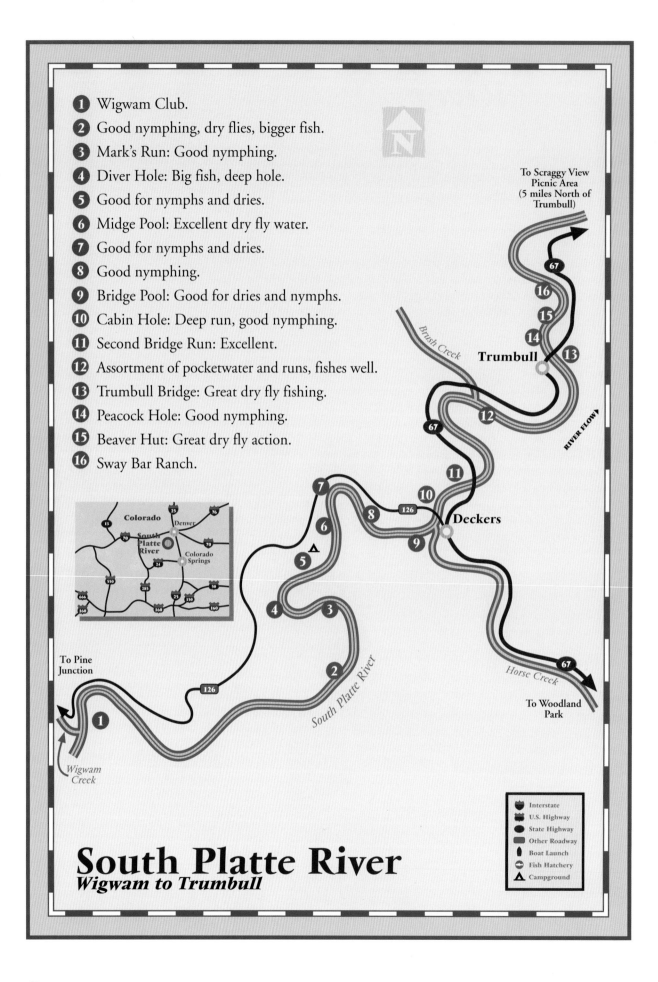

South Platte River
Wigwam to Trumbull

South Platte River
Below the Wigwam Club to Trumbull

Downstream from Cheesman Canyon fly fishers can enjoy another incredible section of the South Platte River. There are usually some 7,000 rainbow trout per mile in this picturesque setting. Access is easier here than the Cheesman Canyon section.

To find this section of the South Platte, drive west from the Denver area on Highway 285 to Pine Junction. Take Highway 126 south approximately twenty miles to the town of Deckers. Here, you can drive parallel to the river on Colorado 67. This dirt road provides continuous access to the river and the Fence Hole. Parking areas along the river are well marked.

View of the Wigwam Club and the South Platte River, some of the finest, and most popular fly fishing water in Colorado. Photo by Lucas Galli.

Types of Fish
Rainbow, brown and cutbow trout averaging 12 inches.

Known Hatches
All Year: Midges (Diptera), most predominant in winter. *March-May & Sept-Nov:* Mayflies, BWO (Baetis). *June-July:* PMD (Ephemerella inermis & infrequens). *August-September:* Tricos. *May-September:* Various Caddis, Stoneflies (Acroneuria pacifica).

Equipment to Use
Rods: 3-5 weight, 8-9'.
Reels: Disc drag suggested.
Line: Floating to match rod weight.
Leaders: 5x to 7x, 9-12'.
Wading: Cold water, no wet wading, wear chest-high breathable waders and felt-soled boots.

Flies to Use
Dries, January-March: Various Midges, Griffith's Gnat, Midge & Biot Emerger, Stalcup's Film-Wing, #20-26. *April-May:* Baetis, Blue Quill, Baetis Parachute, Comparadun, #18-24. *June-July:* PMD Dries & Emergers, Stalcup's CDC Comparadun, AK's Melon Quill, Light Cahill #16-18, Caddis #14-18, Yellow Stimulators #6-8 for Stonefly hatches. *August-September:* Trico Spinner, Emerger Dun #20-24, Ants & Beetles #6-14, various Caddis #14-18, Olive Humpy, Irresistible, Adams, Wulff #16-20. *October-November:* Baetis #18-24. *Nymphs:* Olive, Natural Pheasant Tail #16-24, Olive, Dun & Natural Hare's Ear #16-22, RS-2, Miracle Nymph, Baetis #18-24, all colors Copper John #14-20, Beadhead Barr's Emerger BWO #16-22, Black, Brown, Red, White, & Olive Midge Larva & Pupa #18-26. Downstream towards Trumbull there are more varied and larger bugs. Use above patterns in larger sizes.

When to Fish
As a tailwater this section of the South Platte fishes well year-round. Very cold spells in winter slow the fish and can make fishing difficult.

Seasons & Limits
Open year-round. From the lower boundary of the Wigwam Club to Scraggy View picnic area, fish with artificial flies and lures only. The bag, possession and size limit for trout is two fish, 16" or longer.

Nearby Fly Fishing
Nothing within 1 1/2 hour drive.

Accommodations & Services
There are a few campgrounds in the area. Cabins, restaurants, gas, fly shop, and general store in Deckers.

Rating
Convenience, lots of fish and year-round fly fishing make this section of the South Platte an 8.5.

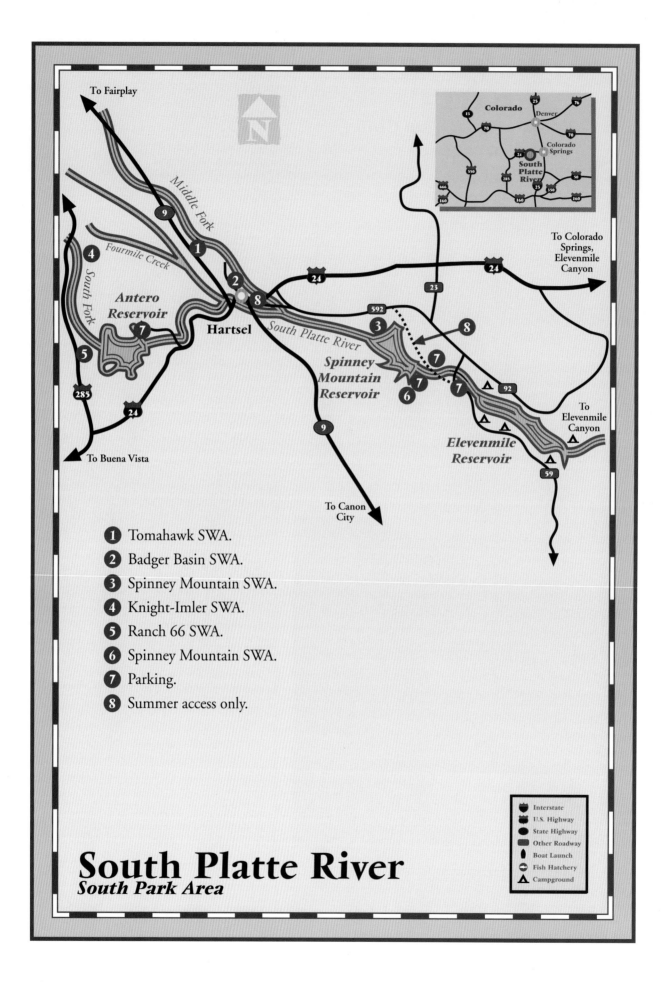

To Fairplay

Middle Fork

Colorado
Denver
Colorado Springs
South Platte River

9

Fourmile Creek

1

4

South Fork

Antero Reservoir

7

5

285

24

To Buena Vista

Hartsel

2

8

24

23

592

3

8

7

6

7

7

92

To Colorado Springs, Elevenmile Canyon

Spinney Mountain Reservoir

South Platte River

9

To Canon City

Elevenmile Reservoir

To Elevenmile Canyon

59

1 Tomahawk SWA.

2 Badger Basin SWA.

3 Spinney Mountain SWA.

4 Knight-Imler SWA.

5 Ranch 66 SWA.

6 Spinney Mountain SWA.

7 Parking.

8 Summer access only.

Interstate
U.S. Highway
State Highway
Other Roadway
Boat Launch
Fish Hatchery
Campground

South Platte River
South Park Area

South Platte River

South Park Area

The oxbow sections of the South Platte flow through a high plain area known as South Park. Over fifty miles of public access to this Gold Medal Water are well marked. Dress for wind and watch for lightning.

Brown trout up to ten pounds migrate up the Middle Fork in the summer. Strikes are spotty but can be worth the effort. Excellent surface fishing to the many summer hatches on the South Fork above and below Antero Reservoir provides great action. Antero was drained in the summer of 2002. At the time this book went to press, the timetable for re-filling the reservoir was not set. Check with CDW.

Below Spinney Mountain Reservoir it's catch and release year-round, with flows of 40-200 cfs. The South and Middle forks of the Platte are small to medium sized. South Fork flows, on average, 15-50 cfs, Middle Fork flows at 30-200 cfs. Green and white signs mark Middle Fork access and are scattered along Highway 9 from Garo to Hartsel.

The Elevenmile Canyon tailwater of the South Platte, now under Forest Service control, is a beautiful canyon that is now producing well. Flows are usually 40-200 cfs. Drive to the town of Lake George and follow the signs.

To reach South Park from the Denver area drive west on Highway 285 to Fairplay; take 285 south for the upper South Fork, or Highway 9 south for the Middle Fork and lower South Fork. From Colorado Springs, take Highway 24 west over Wilkerson Pass.

Middle Fork South Platte River. Photo by Jim Muth.

Types of Fish
Brown trout, Snake River cutthroats, rainbows and brookies. Kokanee below Spinney Mountain Reservoir November-December and northern pike above and in Spinney.

Known Hatches
December-March: Below the reservoirs, Midges (Diptera). *April-May:* Midges, Blue-Winged Olive (Baetis). *June:* PMD (Ephemerella inermis), Golden Stone (Acroneuria pacifica), Caddis. *July:* Midges, Caddis, PMD, Tricos, Yellow Sally (Isoperla). *August-September:* Midges, Caddis, Tricos. *October-November:* Midges, Baetis.

Equipment to Use
Rods: 3-7 weight, 8-9'.
Reels: Palm or mechanical drag.
Line: Floating or sink tip.
Leaders: 0x to 7x, 9-11'.
Wading: Hip boots OK except during spring runoff, otherwise chest-high waders and boots.

Flies to Use
June-July: Light Cahill, PMD Comparadun #16-18, Stimulator #8-10, Elk Hair Caddis, Ants & Beetles, Pink & Lime Trude, Humpy, Irresistible #14-18, Hoppers #12-14, Midges, Renegade #18-20*. *August-September:* To above, add Stimulator #10-14, Beetles & Ants #14-16, Trico Dun & Spinner #18-22*, Baetis #20-22, Adams Parachute #18-20. *October-December:* Midge Emerger & Biot #18-24*, Blue-Winged Olive #20-24, Griffith's Gnats #18-22. *Nymphs & Streamers:* Prince #12-16, Pheasant Tail #16-18*, Copper John #14-20, Beadhead Barr's Emerger BWO #16-22, Woolly Bugger, Flashabugger, Marabou Muddler #2-6, Matuka, Zonker #4-8, Mini Muddler #10-12, Midge Larva, Miracle, WD-40 #18-22*, Brassie #18-20, Scuds, San Juan Worm #14-16*, Gold-Ribbed Hare's Ear (also Beadhead) #14-22, RS-2 #18-24*. *Dries, below Spinney, January-March:* Griffith's Gnat, Midge Biot Emerger, Betts Emerger #18-22. *April-May:* BWO, Parachute Adams #18-20, Elk Hair Caddis #16-18.
*Best below Spinney Mountain Dam

When to Fish
Above Spinney: April to mid-October trout from the reservoirs spawn April-May. Browns migrate from Spinney July-September. Fish below the reservoir year-round, PMD hatch mid-June to mid-July, Tricos August to September Runoff above the reservoir mid-May to June can eliminate fishing. Elevenmile Canyon open year-round.

Seasons & Limits
Regulations vary. Check with a fly shop or the CDW brochure.

Nearby Fly Fishing
The Arkansas and Blue rivers.

Accommodations & Services
Campgrounds at Elevenmile, in the canyon and at Wilkerson Pass. Motels and cabins in Fairplay and Lake George. All services in Hartsel, Fairplay, Lake George and Breckenridge.

Rating
With possibly three tailwaters, various fish and beautiful surroundings, this section is a strong 8.

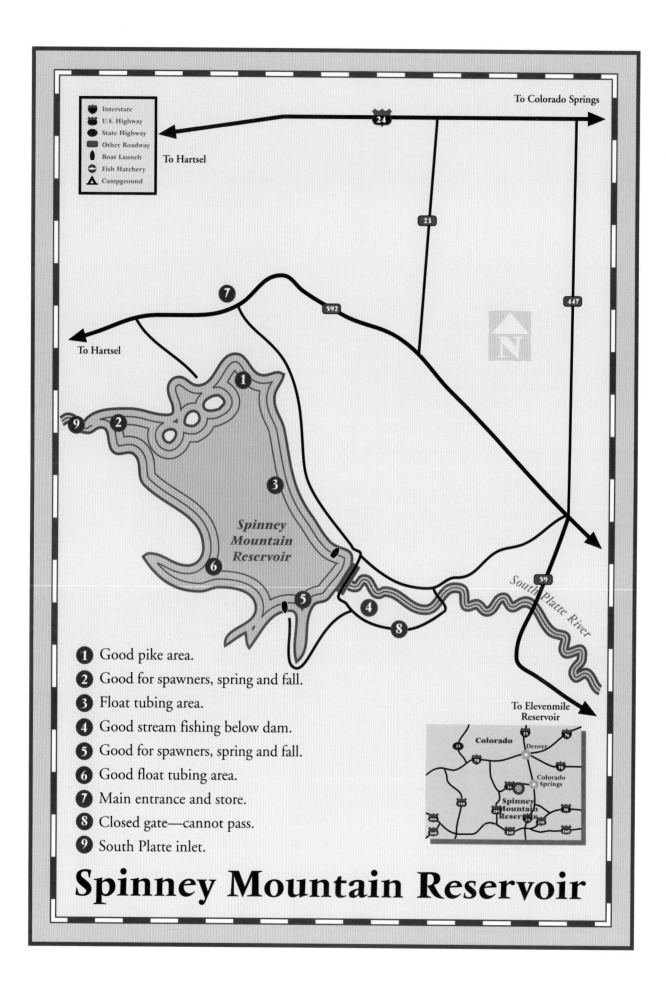

Spinney Mountain Reservoir

To Colorado Springs
To Hartsel
To Hartsel

Legend:
- Interstate
- U.S. Highway
- State Highway
- Other Roadway
- Boat Launch
- Fish Hatchery
- Campground

Spinney
Mountain
Reservoir

South Platte River

To Elevenmile
Reservoir

1 Good pike area.
2 Good for spawners, spring and fall.
3 Float tubing area.
4 Good stream fishing below dam.
5 Good for spawners, spring and fall.
6 Good float tubing area.
7 Main entrance and store.
8 Closed gate—cannot pass.
9 South Platte inlet.

Spinney Mountain Reservoir

Spinney Mountain Reservoir

Spinney Mountain Reservoir (created by the city of Aurora) is one of Colorado's finest lake fisheries. It has given anglers many rewarding days for many years, although recently the lake's production has declined somewhat. All things considered, however, it's still a very good place to fly fish and on any given summer weekend the lake is covered with boats and float tubes filled with anglers catching and releasing fish.

Despite this popularity and heavy pressure, production remains generally good and one should not be discouraged by what appears to be a crowd. Spinney is one of the few reservoirs in Colorado designated a Gold Medal Water.

Types of Fish
Rainbow, brown, Snake River cutthroats and northern pike.

Known Hatches
May-October: Midges.
June-August: Callibaetis.
July-August: Damsels.

Equipment to Use
Rods: 5-8 weight, 9-10'.
Reels: Mechanical or palm drag.
Line: Floating, sinking and sink tip to match rod weight.
Leaders: 1x-5x for trout, steel or 40-50 lb. test for pike.
Wading: Float tubes are preferred for trout fishing. Chest-high waders are recommended for this cold water. Beware of heavy winds.

Flies to Use
Dries, Summer: Adams Parachute #14-16, No-Hackle Callibaetis #16, Damselflies #8-10.
Nymphs: Pheasant Tail, Hare's Ear #12-18, Zug Bug, Muskrat #14-18, all colors Copper John #14-20, Beadhead Barr's Emerger BWO #16-22, Olive & Tan Scud #14-16, Leech, Woolly Bugger, Zonker #2-4, Barr's Damsel Nymph #6-8, Barr's Bouface #2 (for Pike).

When to Fish
The lake closes at first ice and usually opens in early April. Fishing is very good during the opening week. Pike fishing is best from mid-June to mid-July in the afternoon when the wind comes up and when the fish move to the flats to spawn. Fishing on the South Platte inlet in May for the rainbows and cutts is very good. In September, try the same inlet for the spawning browns.

Seasons & Limits
In most years the lake opens in April and closes in November. Fishing is prohibited 1/2 hour after sunset until 1/2 hour before sunrise. Ice fishing is prohibited. Artificial flies and lures only. The bag and possession limit for trout is one fish, 20 inches or longer. Always check at a fly shop and the current regulations brochure. Note: the water level was lowered in 2002. Check with the State Parks office for updates on boat ramp access (719-748-3401).

Nearby Fly Fishing
Middle and South Forks of the South Platte River above and below the reservoir, the Arkansas River and Elevenmile Canyon.

Accommodations & Services
Camping is available at two locations around Elevenmile Reservoir. There is also camping at the Chaparral Park Store & Campground near the entrance to the reservoir. Lodging can be found at Lake George and Fairplay. Services such as gas and groceries are available in Hartsel, Lake George and Fairplay.

Rating
Spinney Mountain is possibly the best reservoir in the state. A fly fisher's ever-present chance to catch a lunker trout and pike makes this water an 8.

Spinney Mountain Rainbow Trout. Photo by Jim Muth.

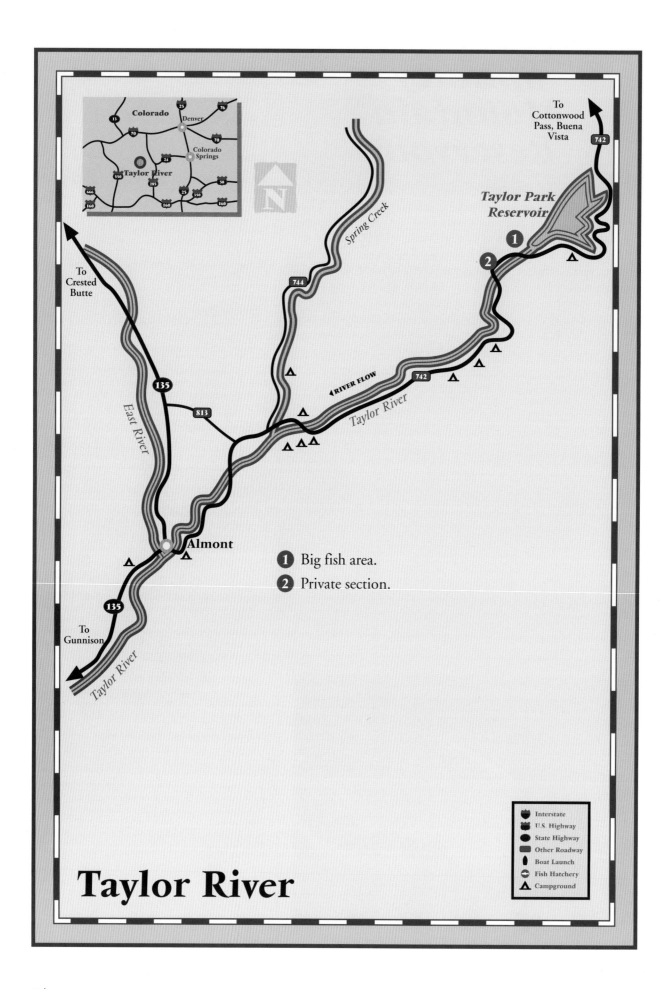

To Cottonwood Pass, Buena Vista
742

Colorado
Denver
Colorado Springs
Taylor River

Taylor Park Reservoir

Spring Creek

744

To Crested Butte

135

813

◀RIVER FLOW

742

Taylor River

East River

Almont

❶ Big fish area.

❷ Private section.

135

To Gunnison

Taylor River

🛢	Interstate
🛡	U.S. Highway
⬭	State Highway
▭	Other Roadway
🚤	Boat Launch
⬭	Fish Hatchery
▲	Campground

Taylor River

Taylor River

This twenty-mile stretch of river flows through a beautiful valley with scenery and water changing around every bend. The Taylor offers fly fishers some interesting opportunities, especially below the dam where a very small public stretch of water holds large rainbow trout. These Mysis shrimp-fed fish, however, are very difficult to hook, let alone land. Downstream past some private water there are smaller fish, but the catching is easier.

This tailwater fishery runs at about 250-300 cfs most of the year and provides year-round fishing near the dam. It's a little out of the way, but if you're in the area don't miss this beautiful spot.

To reach the Taylor River from Buena Vista and Highway 285, drive west over Cottonwood pass. This takes about an hour and involves twenty-five miles of dirt road. From the west or Gunnison, take Highway 135 north to Almont. Turn right in Almont to find the river.

An angler battles with a trout on the Taylor River.
Photo by Ben Furimsky.

Types of Fish
Rainbow and brown trout with more browns downstream.

Known Hatches
April-May & September-October: Mayflies, Baetis. *June, July, August:* Pale Morning Dun (Ephemerella inermis). *August:* Green Drake (Ephemerella grandis). *August-September:* Blue Dun (Cinygmula). *May-August:* variety of Caddis, Stoneflies, Golden Stone (Acroneuria pacifica). *December-February:* Midges (Diptera).

Equipment to Use
Rods: 3-5 weight, 8-9'.
Reels: Mechanical or palm drag.
Line: Floating to match rod weight.
Leaders: 4x to 6x, 9-13'.
Wading: The water is generally quite cold. Wear chest-high waders with felt-soled boots.

Flies to Use
Dries, April-May: Blue-Winged Olive, Baetis Parachute, Midge #18-22. *May:* Over eighteen different Caddis. *August-September:* Green Drake #12, Blue Dun, Pink Cahill #14-16, PMD, Melon Quill, Royal Wulff, Humpy, Irresistible #14-18, Caddis #16-18, Hoppers #12-14, Pink Trude #14-16, Beetles #14. *October-November:* Baetis, Adams & Betts Midge Emerger #18-22. *Nymphs & Streamers:* Mysis Shrimp #16-18, Beadhead Barr's Emerger BWO #16-22, Midge Larva, Brassies #18-20, Pheasant Tail, Kimball's Emerger, Midge Biot, RS-2 #18-22, Beadhead Hare's Ear #16, WD-40 #20-22, all colors Copper John #14-20. *A mile down from the dam try:* Hare's Ear, Prince, Beadhead Caddis #14-18, Pheasant Tail #16-20, Red Squirrel Tail #14-16, Midge Larva #18-20, Woolly Bugger #6-10, Green Drake #12.

When to Fish
The entire river fishes best after runoff, usually July 1 to mid-October. The best dry fly fishing is July-September. The upper river near the dam is open year-round.

Seasons & Limits
Fish year-round. The first 4/10ths of a mile below the dam is catch and release, artificial flies and lures only. The rest of the river is covered by general regulations. Consult the Colorado fishing regulations booklet. Note: the local fly fishing club has a non-wading section below the reservoir. This improves the fishing for all.

Nearby Fly Fishing
The Upper Taylor River, East and Gunnison rivers and Spring, Texas, Willow and Tomichi creeks are all worth investigating.

Accommodations & Services
There are campgrounds around Taylor Park Reservoir and along the river below the dam and cabins and some motels in Almont. There are groceries, gas and restaurants as well. Go to Buena Vista, Gunnison and Crested Butte for all other major services.

Rating
Large fish, lots of fishable water and a pristine setting make the Taylor River an 8.

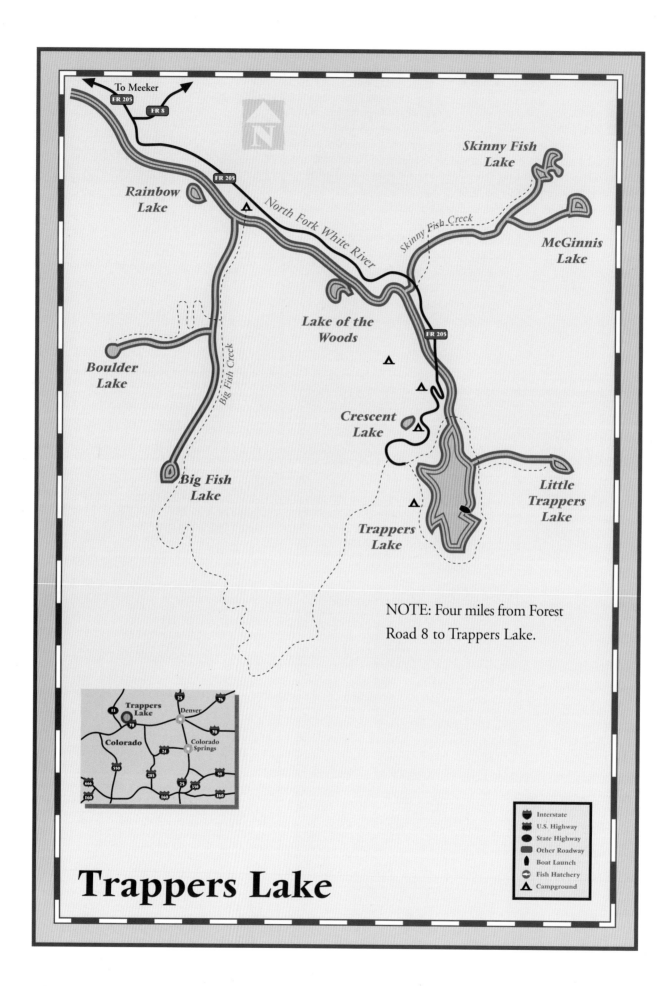

To Meeker

FR 205
FR 8

FR 205

Rainbow Lake

North Fork White River

Skinny Fish Lake

Skinny Fish Creek

McGinnis Lake

Boulder Lake

Big Fish Creek

Lake of the Woods

FR 205

Crescent Lake

Big Fish Lake

Little Trappers Lake

Trappers Lake

NOTE: Four miles from Forest Road 8 to Trappers Lake.

Trappers Lake
13
70
Denver
25
76
Colorado
70
Colorado Springs
550
24
285
25
550
50
666
160
160
160

Interstate
U.S. Highway
State Highway
Other Roadway
Boat Launch
Fish Hatchery
Campground

Trappers Lake

Trappers Lake

Located on the border of the Flat Tops Wilderness Area and at over 10,000 feet elevation, Trappers is one of Colorado's most beautiful natural lakes. The 200 acres of water is home to a wild strain of cutthroat trout and offers the angler productive fishing throughout the summer. This lake is also rated Wild Trout Water and is a fish source for hatcheries around the country.

Many of the more remote areas around the lake are restricted to foot or horse travel only. Canoes and float tubes will help provide access to these areas. Crystal clear waters afford many sight-fishing opportunities. Dry fly fishing can be superb when the lake is calm.

To find Trappers Lake drive west on Interstate 70 to the town of Rifle. Go north on Highway 13 to Meeker. At Meeker go right on Forest Road 8, which parallels the White River. Turn onto Forest Road 205. It's about twenty miles from Meeker to Trappers Lake.

12,002 foot Trappers Peak, to the southwest and above Trappers Lake, seen from the Wall Lake Trail. This trail begins near Trappers Lake and climbs 1,400 feet in three miles. Photo by Al Marlowe, author of A Hiking and Camping Guide to the Flat Tops Wilderness Area.

Types of Fish
Cutthroat trout and brook trout.

Known Hatches
June-September: Midges.
Late-June to July: Damsel.
Mid-July to August: Callibaetis.

Equipment to Use
Rods: 4-5 weight, 8 1/2-9 1/2'.
Reels: Mechanical or palm drag.
Line: Low visibility, floating to match rod weight.
Leaders: 5x - 6x, 9-12'.
Wading: Very little available area, so bring a boat or float tube. Motors are not allowed. There is about a 1/4-mile walk to the lake.

Flies to Use
Dries: Adams and Adams Parachute, Royal Wulff, Irresistible, Adams #14-18, Callibaetis #14-16, Shroeder's Para-Hopper #8-12, Beetles #14, Ants #14-16. *Nymphs & Streamers:* Prince Nymph, Pheasant Tail #12-16, Beadhead Barr's Emerger BWO #16-22, Damsel #8-12, Zug Bug #14-16, all colors Copper John #14-20, Woolly Bugger #6-10.

When to Fish
The best time to fish Trappers Lake is mid-June until late September. Ice-off can come late because of heavy snows and cold temperatures that are normal for this area.

Seasons & Limits
Artificial flies and lures only. The bag and possession limit for cutthroat trout is two fish. All cutthroat greater than 10 inches in length must be returned to the water immediately. Fishing is prohibited in all inlets and upstream in the inlets for one-half mile. Fishing is prohibited within 100 feet of the inlets and outlet streams, in the outlet and downstream to the first falls. There is no limit for brookies. Check current regulations and at a fly shop.

Nearby Fly Fishing
The Flat Tops area has many other lakes and creeks that should not be missed, and the White River is definitely worth fly fishing.

Accommodations & Services
Pay camping is available. Cabins, canoes and rowboats for rent at the recently rebuilt Trappers Lake Lodge. Gas and groceries are also available at the lodge.

Rating
During July, August and September dry fly fishing for wild trout is excellent; I rate it a 9.

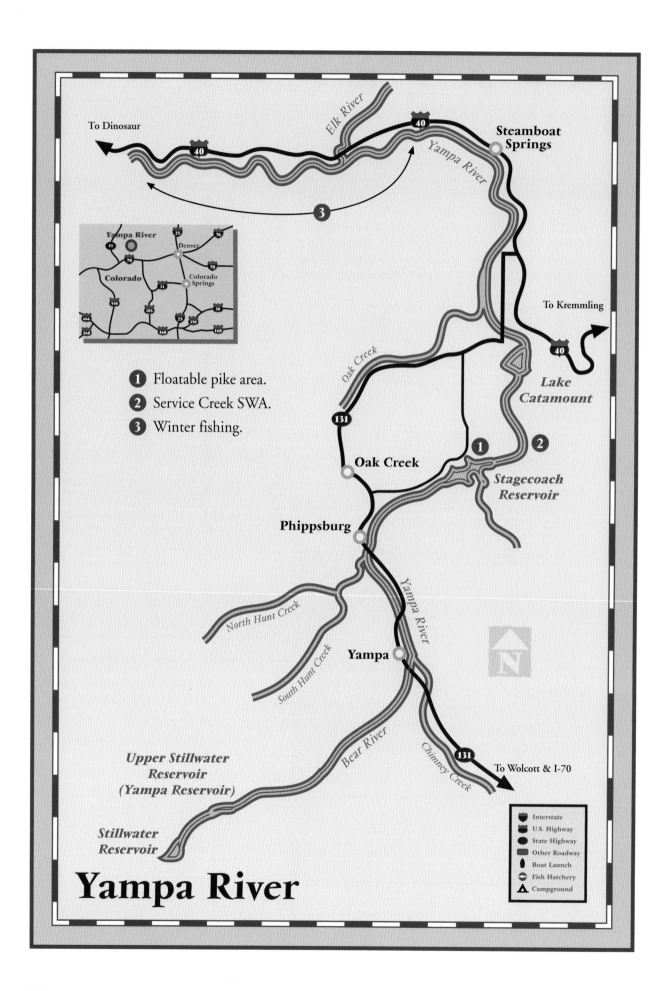

To Dinosaur

Elk River

40

40

Steamboat Springs

Yampa River

Yampa River

3

Yampa River

To Kremmling

40

Lake Catamount

1 Floatable pike area.

2 Service Creek SWA.

3 Winter fishing.

Oak Creek

131

1

2

Stagecoach Reservoir

Oak Creek

Phippsburg

North Hunt Creek

Yampa River

Yampa

South Hunt Creek

N

Bear River

Chimney Creek

131

To Wolcott & I-70

Upper Stillwater Reservoir (Yampa Reservoir)

Stillwater Reservoir

Yampa River

Interstate
U.S. Highway
State Highway
Other Roadway
Boat Launch
Fish Hatchery
Campground

Colorado map inset: Yampa River, Denver, Colorado, Colorado Springs, 13, 25, 76, 70, 24, 550, 285, 25, 50, 50, 160, 160, 666, 160

Yampa River

The Yampa (bear in Native American language) originates high above the northwest Colorado town of Yampa, into which the Bear River flows. Wonderfully varied fly fishing opportunities abound along the 150 river miles of water as it flows west to Dinosaur National Monument and Utah's fabled Green River.

The fifteen-mile stretch from Stillwater Reservoir to Yampa has tailwaters, pretty meadow sections and tumbling freestone waters. Fly fishing for the "Rocky Mountain Grand Slam" (brook, rainbow, cutthroat, brown and whitefish) is quite possible in this section. Fish average 8-16 inches here. The next ten to fifteen miles of river are private until the 1/2 to 3/4 miles upstream of the inlet into Stagecoach Reservoir. Below the reservoir are two public sections of small tailwaters with some beautiful rainbows and cutthroats.

From the Service Creek Wildlife Area downstream to the town of Steamboat Springs (fifteen miles) the river flows through private lands.

You'll be pleased with the river rock and habitat placed along the river through the town of Steamboat Springs. Though angling here is urban fishing, you will still have fun.

From Steamboat Springs west to Craig (fifty miles) the river is large and mostly private making access a problem. Fish for northern pike here. The trout populations begin to thin outside of Craig and are all but gone below Craig. Selected rocky areas from Craig downstream provide good smallmouth bass fishing.

It's best to float the river and the three beautiful canyons from Craig to the monument boundary (40-50 miles). A two or three day trip is best. Access to most of this river is on BLM land and from various local roads off U.S. Highway 40. Check local maps first.

Anglers in the tailwater section of the Yampa River, below Stagecoach Reservoir. Photo by Al Marlowe.

Types of Fish
Rainbow, brown, cutthroat, and brook trout, whitefish, northern pike, smallmouth bass.

Known Hatches
March-May and September-October: Blue-Winged Olive (Baetis). *June-July:* Pale Morning Dun (Ephemerella inermis). *July-August:* Yellow Sally (Isoperla). *June-August:* Various Caddis.

Equipment to Use
Rods: 4-9 weight, 8-9 1/2'.
Reels: Light to medium heavy with good disc drag.
Line: Floating and sink tips to match rod weight.
Leaders: Pike, 0x w/shock tippets. Trout, 3x to 6x, 8-10'.
Wading: Hip boots and wet wading in summer.

Flies to Use
Trout: Attractors: Humpy, Wulff, Irresistible, Trude #12-16. *Nymphs:* Prince, Hare's Ear, Pheasant Tail, Flashback, Regular and Beadhead #2-18, all colors Copper John #14-20, Beadhead Barr's Emerger BWO #16-22. *Streamers:* Zonker, Bugger #2-6. *Terrestrials:* Beetle, Hopper #8-14.
Below Stagecoach: Baetis #18-22, PMD #14-18, Caddis #12-18. *Winter:* Midges #18-22 (mostly larva). *Pike:* Gator Getters, Whistler, Barr's Bouface, Floating Hairbug, Poppers #4/0-#2.

When to Fish
Fish June-November on most of the river. Some winter fishing is available below Stagecoach Reservoir.

Seasons & Limits
Fishing the Yampa is especially good during the spring spawn of 12-24 inch rainbows. The river is open to fishing year-round from the Elk River to Catamount Dam and the bag and possession limit for trout is two fish. From Lake Catamount to Stagecoach Dam, artificial flies and lures only. The bag and possession for trout is two fish.

Nearby Fly Fishing
The Colorado and Elk rivers, Stagecoach Reservoir and Pearl Lake. The Flat Top's lakes area has many spots. Sands Lake is good.

Accommodations & Services
Few campgrounds around Stagecoach Reservoir and Stillwater Reservoir and Upper Stillwater Reservoir. Camping permitted on the BLM sections of the lower river. Numerous campgrounds in the Steamboat area and motels, hotels, B&Bs and condos. Restaurants, groceries and major services are available in most towns along the Yampa.

Rating
Diversity of fish, terrain and habitat make this interesting river an 8.

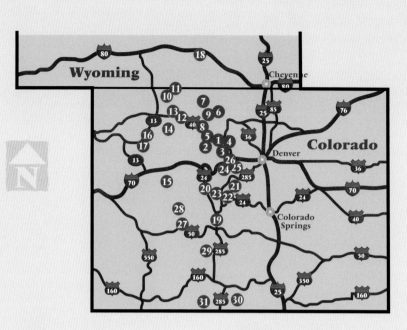

1 Colorado River
2 Lower Muddy Creek
3 Fraser River
4 Ranch Creek & Ponds
5 Kremmling Pond
6 Michigan River
7 North Fork, North Platte
8 Upper Muddy Creek
9 Whistling Elk Ranch
10 Slater Creek
11 Little Snake River
12 Yampa River
13 Steamboat Trout Ranch
14 B.V. Ranch
15 Gianinetti Ranch
16 Coal Creek

17 White River
18 Elk Mountain Lake, WY
19 Arkansas River
20 Lake Fork
21 Tarryall Creek
22 Middle Fork, South Platte
23 Four Mile Creek
24 Silver Valley Lake
25 Clear Creek
26 Empire Lake
27 Gunnison River
28 East River
29 Saguache Creek
30 Culebra Creek
31 Conejos River

Rocky Mountain Angling Club

Interstate
U.S. Highway
State Highway
Other Roadway
Boat Launch
Fish Hatchery
Campground

Rocky Mountain Angling Club

Colorado has one of the best organized offerings of private, under-fished, uncrowded fly fishing waters in the United States. Rocky Mountain Angling Club members enjoy exclusive fishing privileges on the club's forty-six catch and release destinations and a lake in Wyoming. It's called the angler/landowner partnership, and here is how it works:

Member anglers select a fishing water, then call to check availability. All waters are reservation only and, if available, limited numbers of members can fish the property. After paying a rod fee of $40-$110, with the average about $50, anglers post a special marker on the dash of their car when parked at the property. They enter at designated access points and then have the place to themselves for the day. There are afternoon rates, rates for young people, and children are free at most properties.

Rod fees are split between the property owner, to cover the cost of the lease, and the club. The club maintains modest amenities such as steps over barbed wire fences and other bits of upkeep, and manages a web site, reservations system and office. This is open twelve hours a day during the angling season and provides fishing reports, information on hatches, flow rates, availability, recommendations for nearby accommodations and about anything else a fly fisher could want in a single call.

As of this writing, individual or family members pay a one-time initiation fee of $305 and then $90 per year to stay active. Guests are permitted for just the rod fee. Corporate memberships are available that allow authorized employees to join by paying the annual dues. Membership includes detailed maps, directions, property descriptions, property rules, rates, newsletters full of recent fishing reports and other goodies.

Fishing regulations for each tract are frequently more stringent than state regulations. Most waters are managed to provide big, wild trout so catch and release fishing is practiced most of the time. Bait fishing is not permitted and most waters allow only barbless flies or lures.

Club members keep the areas pristine and fastidiously clean up after themselves. There are no toilet facilities. Only a few leases permit camping, and there are often campsites near many club waters. The property owners often benignly patrol to ensure that only members do the fishing and to keep the area in the preferred state of wilderness.

Information
Rocky Mountain Angling Club
3805 Marshall Street, Suite 303
Wheat Ridge, CO 80033
Phone: 303-421-6239
Toll Free: 800-524-1814
Fax: 303-421-4807
www.rmangling.com
E-mail: rmangling@aol.com

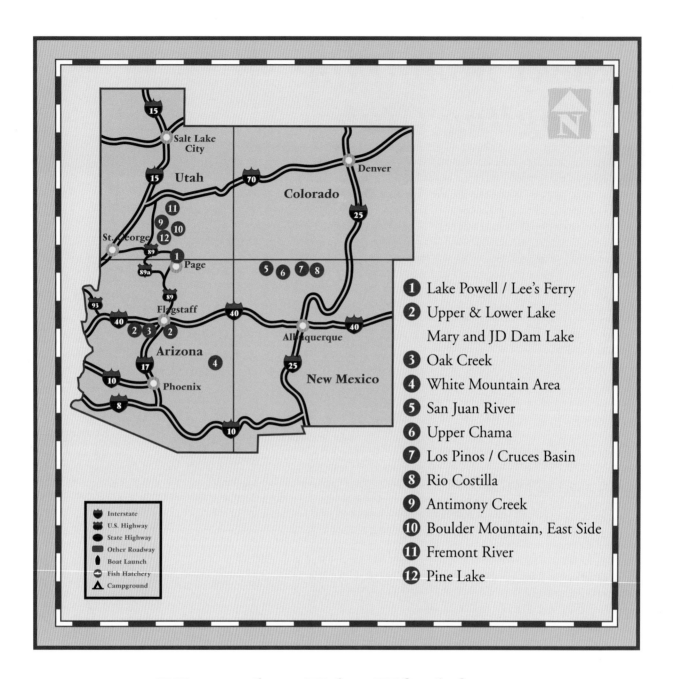

1. Lake Powell / Lee's Ferry
2. Upper & Lower Lake Mary and JD Dam Lake
3. Oak Creek
4. White Mountain Area
5. San Juan River
6. Upper Chama
7. Los Pinos / Cruces Basin
8. Rio Costilla
9. Antimony Creek
10. Boulder Mountain, East Side
11. Fremont River
12. Pine Lake

Nearby Fly Fishing

Many fly waters just outside Colorado are well worth the long drive. Some are diversions while traveling somewhere else. If driving from Colorado, getting to the waters mentioned here should be classified under the heading "Road Trip"!

Information comes from the No Nonsense Fly Fishing Guidebooks series (www.nononsenseguides.com). Thanks to contributing authors, Jackson Streit (CO), Taylor Streit (NM), Steve Schmidt (UT), Glenn Tinnin (AZ), Dave Foster (Lee's Ferry) and editor & publisher David Banks. Map by Pete Chadwell.

Arizona

1. Lake Powell / Lee's Ferry

Powell is huge and best covered with a bass boat. Fish for bass, crappie, carp, walleye, pike and sunfish. Access from Page. Mike Ritz (928) 645-2287, Stix Bait & Tackle (928) 645-2891.

The Colorado River at Lee's Ferry has some walk-in angling, but it's best to go with a guide and a boat. Lots of trout in a magnificent canyon setting. Dave Foster, Marble Canyon Outfitters (800) 533-7339. Terry Gunn, Lee's Ferry Anglers (800) 962-9755.

2. Upper & Lower Lake Mary and JD Dam Lake

Trout and pike available if you are in the area at the right time of day. Fish the weed beds and underwater structure from a kick boat. Babbits, Flagstaff (520) 779-3235, Lynx Creek Unlimited, Prescott (520) 776-7088, Lake Mary Boat Rentals, Flagstaff (520) 774-1742.

3. Oak Creek

Just north of Sedona there are several miles of fishable water with good trout in the upper canyon section. Babbits, Flagstaff (520) 779-3253, Lynx Creek Unlimited, Prescott (520) 776-7088.

4. White Mountain Area

Fish for Apache, rainbow and brown trout and try the Black River, Crescent Lake, Earl Park Lake, the Little Colorado River, the many White Mountain Lakes and the White River. Mountain Outfitters, Pinetop (520) 367-6200, Skier's Edge, Pinetop (520)367-6200.

New Mexico

5. San Juan River

A premier fly fishing destination for tiny flies, light tippets and big fish. Most drift nymphs, though there's excellent sight fishing. Bring waders and warm clothes for cold water. Fox Creek Store, Antonito, CO (719) 376-5881, Abe's Motel & Fly Shop, Navajo Dam, NM (505) 632-2194, Float'n Fish, Navajo Dam, NM (505) 632-5385, New Sportsman Inn, Navajo Dam (505) 632-3271.

6. Upper Chama

Usually best July 1 to early October. Go to Wolf Creek just above the town of Chama for a rugged walk in for big fish from the west side. Easier dry fly fishing just below Chama. Los Rios Anglers, Taos (505) 758-2798, Starr Angler, Red River (505) 754-2320, Williams Trading Post, Red River (505) 754-2217, Taylor Streit Fly Fishing (505) 751-1312.

7. Los Pinos / Cruces Basin

A long drive from anywhere. The stream is seldom over waist deep and has perfect dry fly water. A scenic railroad parallels the water. The Cruces Basin Wilderness Area features a long, dusty ride, brook trout, three creeks, waterfalls, beaver ponds and solitude. Los Rios Anglers, Taos (505) 758-2798, Starr Angler, Red River (505) 754-2320, Williams Trading Post, Red River (505) 754-2217, Taylor Streit Fly Fishing (505) 751-1312.

8. Rio Costilla

Go four miles past Latir Creek for the best water. The meadows of the Valle Vidal unit is the most popular section. Fish for cutthroat Friday-Sunday when water is low. Other times, flows are high for irrigation so stick to edges and slower pools. Try nearby Little Comanche Creek for dry fly action. Cottonwood Meadows, Antonito, CO (719) 376-5660, Hi Country Flies, Trinidad, CO (719) 846-6900, Los Rios Anglers, Taos (505) 758-2798, Taylor Streit Fly Fishing (505) 751-1312.

Utah

9. Antimony Creek

A beautiful little freestone stream, great for dry fly fishing with small rods for wild, 10-16" trout. An OK dirt road leads to Antimony. Fish below Poison Creek and the Sevier River. The trail up a narrow sandstone canyon is very pleasant. Red Rocks Fly Shop, St. George (435) 656-4665, Boulder Mt. Fly Fishing, Boulder (435) 335-7306.

10. Boulder Mountain, East Side

Use scenic Highway 12 to Long Lake and Oak Creek Reservoir and a trailhead for hikes to several lakes. 4WD on Road 179 to Green Lake or to the trailhead to Blind Lake. Several other lakes are within thirty- to ninety-minute hikes. Boulder Mt. Fly Fishing, Boulder (435) 335-7306, Red Rocks Fly Shop, St. George (435) 656-4665.

11. Fremont River

The upper Fremont offers nine miles of fishing along scenic Highway 25. For the best dry fly fishing, head south of Bicknell for very clear water. Western Rivers Flyfishers, Salt Lake City (800) 545-4312, Red Rocks Fly Shop, St. George (435) 656-4665, Boulder Mt. Fly Fishing, Boulder (435) 335-7306.

12. Pine Lake

Take Highway 12 near Bryce Canyon National Park to Highway 63 and head north on Jones Valley Road, then FR 132 and take a right. Use a float tube, canoe, or small boat, especially midday. Fish drop-offs, ledges, and floating weed beds. Boulder Mt. Fly Fishing, Boulder (435) 335-7306, Western Rivers Flyfishers, Salt Lake City (800) 545-4312, Red Rocks Fly Shop, St. George (435) 656-4665.

Resources

Colorado Fly Shops

Mountains

Mountain Angler
P.O. Box 467
311 S. Main St.
Breckenridge, CO 80424
(970) 453-4665
www.mountainangler.com

Alpine Angling
981 Cowen Dr., #A
Carbondale, CO 81623
(970) 963-9245

Blue River Anglers
209 N. Main St.
Breckenridge, CO 80424
(970) 453-9171

Breckenridge Outfitters
100 N. Main St., #205–206
Breckenridge, CO 80424
(970) 453-4135
www.breckenridgeoutfitters.com

Copper Mountain
235 Ten Mile Circle
Copper Mountain, CO 80443
(970) 262-2878

Cutthroat Anglers
400 Blue River Pkwy.
Silverthorne, CO 80498
(970) 262-2878

Eagle River Anglers
25 Eby Creek Rd.
Eagle, CO 81631
(970) 328-2323

Fly Fishing Outfitters
1060 W. Beaver Creek Blvd.
Avon, CO 81620
(970) 476-FISH
www.flyfishingoutfitters.net

Frying Pan Anglers
123 Emma Rd., #100
Basalt, CO 81621
(970) 927-3441

Gore Creek Fly Fisherman
183 E. Gore Creek Rd., #7
Vail, CO 81657
(970) 476-3296

Gorsuch Outfitters
0097 Main St., #E-102
Edwards, CO 81632
(970) 926-0900

Roaring Fork Anglers
2114 #B Grand Ave.
Glenwood Springs, CO 81601
(970) 945-0180

Taylor Creek Angling
183 Basalt Center Circle
Basalt, CO 81621
(970) 927-4374

Taylor Creek Aspen
408 E. Cooper Ave.
Aspen, CO 81611
(970) 920-1128

West

Cimarron Creek Fly Shop
317 East Main St.
Montrose, CO 81401
(970) 249-0408

Dragonfly Anglers
307 Elk Ave.
Crested Butte, CO 81224
(970) 349-1228

Gene Taylor's
445 W. Gunnison
Grand Junction, CO 81505
(970) 242-8165

Gunnison River Pleasure Park
2810 Lane Rd.
Lazear, CO 81420
(970) 872-2525

High Mountain Drifter
115 S. Wisconsin St.
Gunnison, CO 81230
(970) 641-4243

Rigs Fly Shop
565 Sherman Ste. 2
Ridgway, CO 81432
(970) 626-4460
www.fishrigs.com

Three Rivers Fly Shop
130 County Rd. 742
Almont, CO 81210
(970) 641-1303

Western Anglers
2454 Highway 6 & 50 #103
Grand Junction, CO 81505
(970) 244-8658

South

Anasazi Angler
12895 Highway 140
Hesperus, CO 81326
(970) 385-4665

Animas Valley Anglers
1604 W. Third Ave.
Durango, CO 81301
(970) 259-0484

Arkanglers Fly Shop
545 N. Highway 24
Buena Vista, CO 81211
(719) 395-1796

Doc's Outdoor Sports
31101 W. Highway 160
South Fork, CO 81154
(719) 873-5151

Dan's Fly Shop
723 Gunnison Ave.
Lake City, CO 81235
(970) 944-2281

Duranglers
923 Main Ave.
Durango, CO 81301
(970) 385-4081

Durango Fly Goods
139 E. Fifth St.
Durango, CO 81301
(970) 259-0999

One of the many fly fishing waters in the Flat Tops Wilderness. Photo by Jim Muth.

Elk Valley Fly Shop
5535 Highway 12
Laveta, CO 81055
(719) 742-5533

Fox Creek Store
26573 Highway 17
Antonito, CO 81120
(719) 376-5881

Rainbow Sporting Goods
30359 W. US 160
South Fork, CO 81154
(719) 873-5545

Rio Grande Angler
13 S. Main St.
Creede, CO 81130
(719) 658-2955

Royal Gorge Anglers
1210 Royal Gorge Blvd., #1
Canon City, CO 81212
(719) 269-3474

Ski & Bow Rack
354 E. Pagosa St.
Pagosa Springs, CO 81147
(970) 264-2370

The Sportsman Outdoors & Fly Shp
238 S. Gunnison
Lake City, CO 81235
(970) 944-2526

Telluride Angler
121 West Colorado Ave.
Telluride, CO 81435
(970) 728-3895

Telluride Sports
162 Society Dr.
Telluride, CO 81435
(970) 728-4477

Wolf Creek Anglers
001 Brown Ave.
South Fork, CO 81154
(719) 873-1414

Central

Anglers Covey
917 W. Colorado Ave.
Colorado Springs, CO 80905
(719) 471-2984

Arkansas River Fly Shop
7500 West Highway 50
Salida, CO 81201
(719) 539-3474

Colorado Springs Angler
3314 Austin Bluffs Pkwy.
Colorado Springs, CO 80918
(719) 531-5413

Peak Fly Shop
5767 N. Academy Blvd.
Colorado Springs, CO 80918
(719) 260-1415

Plum Creek Anglers
11 Wilcox St.
Castle Rock, CO 80104
(303) 814-0868

T & M Sporting Goods
2023 Lakeview Ave.
Pueblo, CO 81004
(719) 564-0790

North

Anglers Roost
Fort Collins, CO 80524
(970) 377-3785

Bucking Rainbow Outfitters
729 Lincoln Ave.
Steamboat Springs, CO 80477
(970) 879-4693

Buggywhips at Blue Sky West
435 Lincoln Ave.
Steamboat Springs, CO 80477
(970) 879-8033

Estes Angler
338 W. Riverside Dr.
Estes Park, CO 80517
(970) 586-2110

Garretson's Sport Center
3817 W. 10th St.
Greeley, CO 80634
(970) 353-8068

Great Western Fly Fishing Co.
2180 W. Eisenhower, #B
Loveland, CO 80537
(970) 461-0701

Hatch Fly Shop
34375 U.S. Highway 285
Pine, CO 80470
(303) 816-0487

Jax Surplus & Sporting Goods
1200 N. College
Fort Collins, CO 80524
(970) 482-2821

Lyon's Angler
455 Old St. Vrain Rd.
Lyons, CO 80541
(303) 817-3348

Nelson Fly & Tackle
Highway 40
Tabernash, CO 80478
(970) 726-8558

St. Peter's Fly Shop
202 Remington St.
Fort Collins, CO 80524
(970) 498-8968

St. Vrain Angler
418 Main St.
Longmont, CO 80501
(303) 651-6061

Steamboat Fishing Co.
635 Lincoln Ave.
Steamboat Springs, CO 80477
(970) 879-6552

Straightline Fly Shop
744 Lincoln Ave.
Steamboat Springs, CO 80477
(970) 879-7568

Three Forks Ranch
Routt County Rd. 129
Slater, CO 81653
(970) 583-7396

Two Guys Fly Shop
705 S. Public Rd.
Lafayette, CO 80026
(303) 666-7866

Boulder Area
Flatiron Fishing Co.
1 West Flatiron Cir., #356
Broomfield, CO 80021
(303) 439-9219

Front Range Anglers
629 B South Broadway
Boulder, CO 80305
(303) 494-1375

KDE Fly Fishing Co.
275 Brookside Court
Boulder, CO 80302
(303) 415-1100
www.flyfishingflies.com

Kinsley Outfitters, Orvis
1155 13th St.
Boulder, CO 80302
(303) 442-6204

McGuckin Hardware
2525 Arapahoe Ave.
Boulder, CO 80302
(303) 443-1822

Rocky Mt. Anglers
1904 Arapahoe Ave.
Boulder, CO 80302
(303) 447-2400

Denver Area
All Pro Fish 'N Sport
6221 S. Santa Fe Dr.
Littleton, CO 80120
(303) 795-3474

Alpine Angler
2390 S. Chambers Rd.
Aurora, CO 80014
(303) 873-6997

Anglers All
5211 S. Santa Fe Dr.
Littleton, CO 80120
(303) 794-1104

Blue Quill Angler
1532 Bergen Parkway
Evergreen, CO 80439
(303) 674-4700
www.bluequillangler.com

Colorado Angler
1457 Nelson
Lakewood, CO 80215
(303) 232-8298

The Complete Angler
9616 East Arapahoe Rd.
Greenwood Village, CO 80112
(303) 858-8436

Denver Anglers
5455 W. 38th Ave., #E
Denver, CO 80212
(303) 403-4512

Discount Fishing Tackle
2645 S. Santa Fe Dr.
Denver, CO 80223
(303) 698-2550

Flies & Lies
(On the S. Platte, Deckers)
8570 S. Highway 67
Sedalia, CO 80135
(303) 647-2237

Flyfisher, Ltd.
120 Madison St.
Denver, CO 80206
(303) 322-5014

Gart Bros. Sports Castle
1000 Broadway
Denver, CO 80201
(303) 861-1122

Hatch Fly Shop of Evergreen
32214 Ellingwood Trail
Evergreen, CO 80439
(303) 674-0482

High Country Bass'n Shop
1126 S. Sheridan Blvd.
Denver, CO 80232
(303) 934-4156

Orvis Company Store
Centennial Promenade
Englewood, CO 80112
(303) 768-9600

Rick's Rods
2066 S. Huron St.
Denver, CO 80223
(303) 778-7911

River & Stream Co.
Southglenn Mall
6911 S. University Blvd.
Centennial, CO 80123
(303) 794-7864

Royal Steven's Ltd.
1610 E. Girard Pl., #I
Englewood, CO 80113
(303) 788-0433

Tackle Box
4804 Morrison Rd.
Denver, CO 80219

The Trout Fisher
2020 S. Parker Rd.
Denver, CO 80231
(303) 369-7970

Trout's Drygoods & Flyfishing
1069 S. Gaylord St.
Denver, CO 80209
(303) 733-1434

Uncle Milty's Tackle Box
4811 S. Broadway
Englewood, CO 80110
(303) 789-3775

Colorado Fishing Conditions
Northeast: (303) 291-7536
Southeast: (303) 291-7538
Northwest: (303) 291-7537
Denver & Foothills:
(303) 291-7536
Southwest: (303) 291-7539

USGS Stream Flow Information
waterdata.usgs.gov/co/nwis

Division of Wildlife Recorded Fishing Reports
Information:
(303) 291-7533
Fish stocking:
(303) 291-7534

Colorado Division of Wildlife (DOW) Fishing Season Information Booklet
Headquarters and
Central Region
6060 Broadway
Denver, CO 80216
(303) 297-1192

DOW Fort Collins
317 W. Prospect Ave.
Fort Collins, CO 80526
(970) 472-4300

DOW West Region
711 Independent Ave.
Grand Junction, CO 81505
(970) 255-6100

DOW Southeast Region
4255 Sinton Rd.
Colorado Springs, CO
80907
(719) 227-5200

DOW Montrose
2300 S. Townsend
Montrose, CO 81401
(970) 252-6000

Bureau of Land Management
2850 Youngfield St.
Lakewood, CO 80215
(303) 239-3600

U.S. Forest Service
740 Simms St.
Golden, CO 80401
(303) 275-5350
www.ff.fed.us

Parks & Outdoor Recreation
Boating Laws & Safety/State
Lands & Parks
1313 Sherman St., #618
Denver, CO 80203
(303) 866-3437
www.parks.state.co.us

Rocky Mountain National Park
Estes Park, CO 80517
(970) 586-1206
www.nps.gov

Colorado Ski Country USA
1507 Blake St.
Denver, CO 80202
(303) 837-0793

References and Other Reading
Bureau of Reclamation Lakes Guide
Roundabout Publications

Colorado Fishing Season Information & Property Directory
Colorado Division of
Wildlife
www.hps.gov

Colorado Atlas And Gazetteer
Delorme Mapping

Colorado Angling Guide
Streamstalker Publications

Colorado Outdoors Fishing Guide
Colorado Division of
Wildlife

Colorado Trout Fishing Video
Colorado Division of
Wildlife

Illustrated Guide to the Mountain Stream Insects of Colorado
University Press of Colorado

Tim Kelly's Colorado Fishing, Hunting & Outdoor Guide
Hart Publications

Fly Fishing the South Platte River
Pruett Publishing

Fly Fishing the Rocky Mountain Backcountry
Stackpole Books

Fly Fishing Guide for the Roaring Fork Valley
Shook Book Publishing

Western Streamside Guide
Amato Publications

Colorado Fly Fishing Clubs
Colorado Trout Unlimited
1320 Pearl St., #320
Boulder, CO 80302
(303) 440-2937

Boulder Fly Casters
P.O. Box 541
Boulder, CO 80302

Front Range Fly Fishers
P.O. Box 46112
Denver, CO 80201

Gunnison Angling Society
109 Irwin St.
Gunnison, CO 81230

High Plains Fly Drifters
P.O. Box 380386
Denver, CO 80238

Pikes Peak Fly Fishers
2103 E. Greenwich Circle
Colorado Springs, CO
80909

Colorado Women Fly Fishers
P.O. Box 46035
Denver, CO 80201

Fly Fishing Organizations
Federation of Fly Fishers National Headquarters
www.fedflyfishers.org

International Game Fish Association
300 Gulf Stream Way
Dania Beach, FL 33004
(954) 927-2628
www.igfa.org

National Fresh Water Fishing Hall of Fame
P.O. Box 690
Hayward, WI 54843
(715) 634-4440
www.freshwater-fishing.org

Fly Fishing The Internet
www.fedflyfishers.org
www.tu.org
www.flyshop.com
www.flyfishamerica.com
www.flyfishing.com
www.ohwy.com
www.amrivers.org
www.gorp.com

Conservation

No Nonsense Fly Fishing Guidebooks believes that, in addition to local information and gear, fly fishers need clean water and healthy fish. We encourage preservation, improvement, conservation, enjoyment and understanding of our waters and their inhabitants. While fly fishing, take care of the place, practice catch and release and try to avoid spawning fish.

When you aren't fly fishing, a good way to help all things wild and aquatic is to support organizations dedicated to these ideas. No Nonsense Fly Fishing Guidebooks does, and is a member, sponsor of, and donor to organizations that preserve what we cherish. We encourage you to get involved, learn more and to join such organizations.

American Fly Fishing Trade Association .... (360) 636-0708
American Rivers .... (202) 347-7550
California Trout .... (415) 392-8887
Deschutes Basin Land Trust .... (541) 330-0017
Ducks Unlimited .... (901) 758-3825
Federation of Fly Fishers .... (406) 585-7592
International Game Fish Association .... (954) 941-3474
International Women Fly Fishers .... (925) 934-2461
New Mexico Trout .... (505) 344-6363
Oregon Trout .... (503) 222-9091
Outdoor Writers Association of America .... (406) 728-7434
Recreational Fishing Alliance .... (888) JOIN-RFA
Rails-to-Trails Conservancy .... (202) 331-9696
Theodore Roosevelt Conservation Partnership .... (877) 770-8722
Trout Unlimited .... (800) 834-2419

Find Your Way With These No Nonsense Guides

Business Traveler's Guide To Fly Fishing The Western States
Bob Zeller

A seasoned road warrior reveals where one can fly fish within a two hour drive of every major airport in thirteen western states. Don't miss another day fishing!
ISBN #1-892469-01-4 .... $18.95

A Woman's Guide To Fly Fishing Favorite Waters
Yvonne Graham

Forty-five of the top women fly fishing experts reveal their favorite waters. From scenic spring creeks in the East, big trout waters in the Rockies to exciting Baja: all described from the female perspective. A major donation goes to Casting for Recovery, a nonprofit organization for women recovering from breast cancer.
ISBN #1-892469-03-0 .... $19.95

Fly Fishing Southern Baja
Gary Graham

With this book you can fly to Baja, rent a car and go out on your own to find exciting saltwater fly fishing! Mexico's Baja Peninsula is now one of the premier destinations for saltwater fly anglers.
ISBN #1-892469-00-6 .... $18.95

Fly Fishing Arizona
Glenn Tinnin

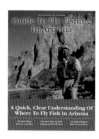

Desert, forest, lava fields, red rocks and canyons. Here is where to go and how to fish 32 streams, lakes, bass waters, reservoirs and saltwater fly fishing Rocky Point, Mexico (a favorite getaway from Phoenix).
ISBN #1-892469-02-2 .... $18.95

Fly Fishing Idaho
Bill Mason

The Henry's Fork, Salmon, Snake and Silver Creek plus 24 other waters. Mr. Mason penned the first fly fishing guidebook to Idaho in 1994. It was updated in 1996 and showcases Bill's 30 plus years of Idaho fly fishing.
ISBN #0-9637256-1-0 .... $14.95

Fly Fishing Utah
Steve Schmidt

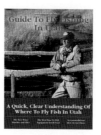

Utah yields extraordinary, uncrowded and little known fishing. Steve Schmidt, outfitter and owner of Western Rivers Fly Shop in Salt Lake City has explored these waters for over 28 years. Fly fishing mountain streams and lakes, tailwaters, bass waters and reservoirs.
ISBN #0-9637256-8-8 .... $19.95

Fly Fishing Nevada
Dave Stanley

The Truckee, Walker, Carson, Eagle, Davis, Ruby, mountain lakes and more. Mr. Stanley is recognized nationwide as the most knowledgeable fly fisher and outdoorsman in the state of Nevada. He owns and operates the Reno Fly Shop and Truckee River Outfitters in Truckee, California.
ISBN #0-9637256-2-9 .... $18.95

Fly Fishing Pyramid Lake Nevada
Terry Barron

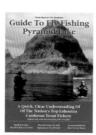

The Gem of the Desert is full of huge Lahontan Cutthroat trout. Terry has recorded everything you need to fly fish the most outstanding trophy cutthroat fishery in the U.S. Where else can you get tired of catching 18-25" trout?
ISBN #0-9637256-3-7 .... $15.95

90

Fly Fishing Magdalena Bay
Gary Graham

Guide and excursion leader Gary Graham (Baja On The Fly) lays out the truth about fly fishing for snook in mangroves, off-shore marlin, calving whales from Alaska, beautiful birds, kayaking, even surfing. Photos, illustrations, maps, and travel information, this is "the Bible" for this unique region.
ISBN #1-892469-08-1 .... $24.95

Fly Fishing Lee's Ferry
Dave Foster

This colorful guide provides a clear understanding of the complex and fascinating 15 miles of river that can provide fly anglers 40-fish days. Detailed maps direct fly and spin fishing access. Learn history, boating and geology and see the area's beauty. Indispensable for the angler and intrepid visitor to the Marble Canyon.
ISBN #1-892469-07-3 .... $21.95

Seasons of the Metolius
John Judy

This new book describes how a beautiful riparian environment both changes and stays the same over the years. This look at nature comes from a man who makes his living working in nature and chronicles John Judy's 30 years of study, writing and fly fishing his beloved home water, the crystal clear Metolius River in central Oregon.
ISBN #1-892469-11-1 .... $21.95

Fly Fishing Central and Southeastern Oregon
Harry Teel

Coming Soon: The Metolius, Deschutes, McKenzie, Owyhee, John Day & 35 other waters. Mr. Teel's 60 years of fly fishing went into the first No Nonsense fly fishing guide, published in 1993 and updated, expanded and improved in 1998 by Jeff Perin. Now updated again and bigger and better than ever.
ISBN #1-892469-09-X $19.95

Fly Fishing California
Ken Hanley

Coming Soon: Mr. Hanley and some very talented contributors like Jeff Solis, Dave Stanley, Katie Howe and others, have fly fished nearly every top water in California. Saltwater, bass, steelhead, high mountains, they provide all you need to discover the best places to fly fish in the Golden State.
ISBN #1-892469-10-3 .... $19.95

Colorado River at sunset. Photo by Jim Muth.

Fly Fishing Knots

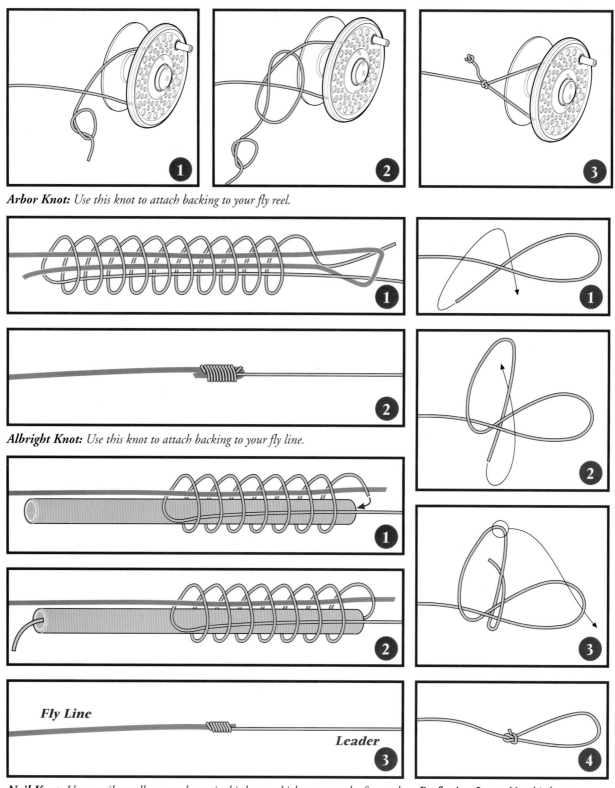

Arbor Knot: *Use this knot to attach backing to your fly reel.*

Albright Knot: *Use this knot to attach backing to your fly line.*

Fly Line

Leader

Nail Knot: *Use a nail, needle or a tube to tie this knot, which connects the forward end of the fly line to the butt end of the leader. Follow this with a Perfection Loop and you've got a permanent end loop that allows easy leader changes.*

Perfection Loop: *Use this knot to create a loop in the butt end of the leader for loop-to-loop connections.*

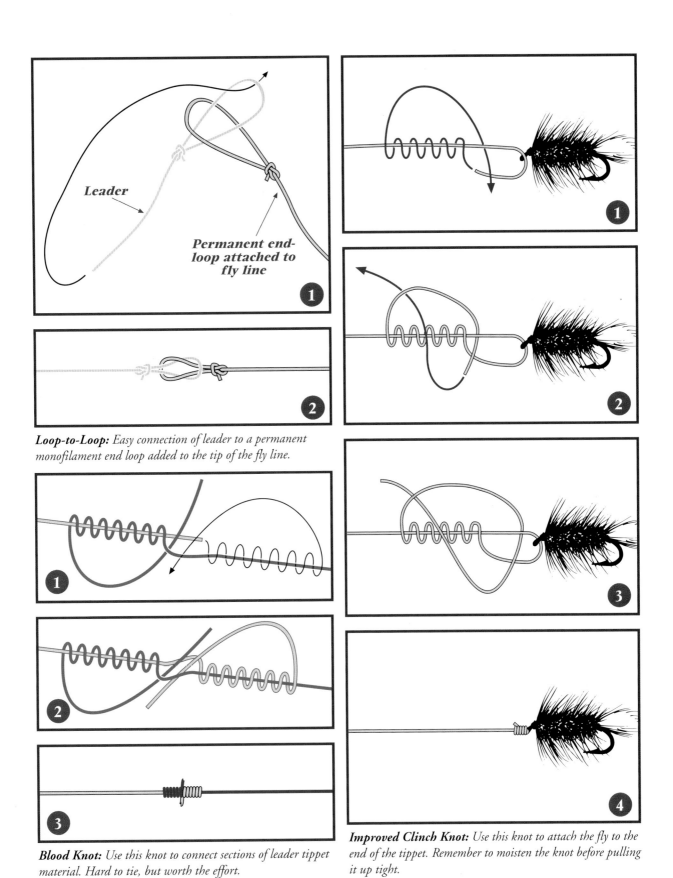

Loop-to-Loop: *Easy connection of leader to a permanent monofilament end loop added to the tip of the fly line.*

Blood Knot: *Use this knot to connect sections of leader tippet material. Hard to tie, but worth the effort.*

Improved Clinch Knot: *Use this knot to attach the fly to the end of the tippet. Remember to moisten the knot before pulling it up tight.*

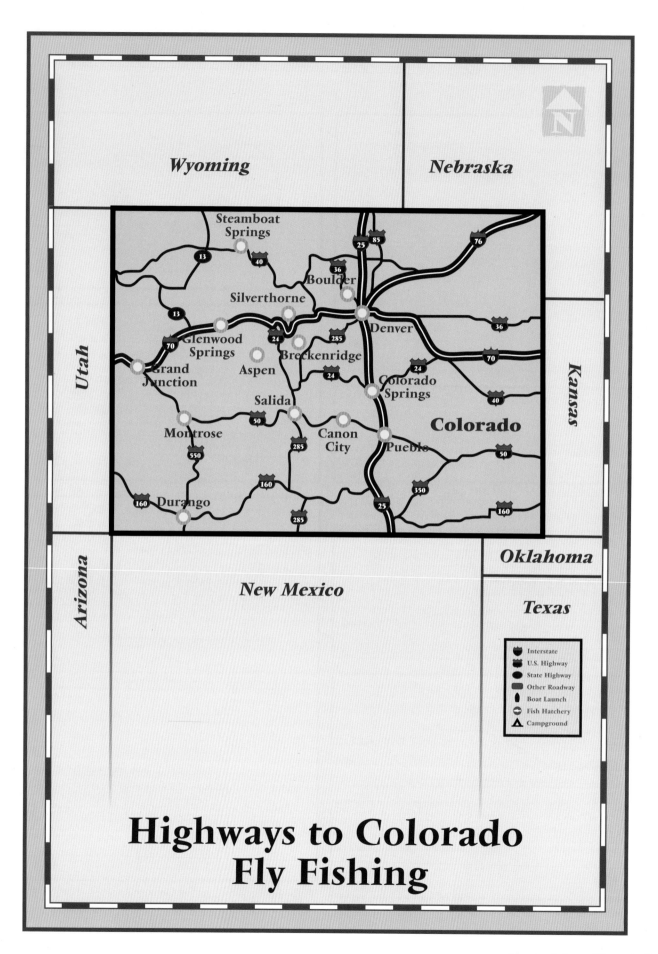

Highways to Colorado Fly Fishing

Floating Spinney Mountain Reservoir.
Photo by Jim Muth.

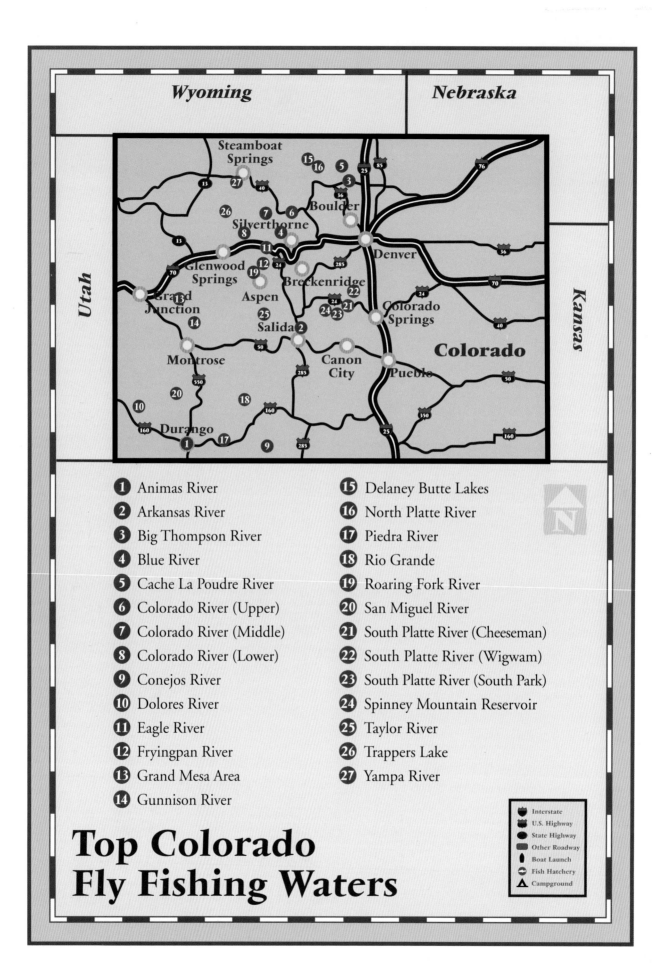

1	Animas River	**15**	Delaney Butte Lakes
2	Arkansas River	**16**	North Platte River
3	Big Thompson River	**17**	Piedra River
4	Blue River	**18**	Rio Grande
5	Cache La Poudre River	**19**	Roaring Fork River
6	Colorado River (Upper)	**20**	San Miguel River
7	Colorado River (Middle)	**21**	South Platte River (Cheeseman)
8	Colorado River (Lower)	**22**	South Platte River (Wigwam)
9	Conejos River	**23**	South Platte River (South Park)
10	Dolores River	**24**	Spinney Mountain Reservoir
11	Eagle River	**25**	Taylor River
12	Fryingpan River	**26**	Trappers Lake
13	Grand Mesa Area	**27**	Yampa River
14	Gunnison River		

Top Colorado
Fly Fishing Waters

Interstate
U.S. Highway
State Highway
Other Roadway
Boat Launch
Fish Hatchery
Campground